The China Sinkhole

Increasing systemic fragility underneath China's debt-laden economy, expedited by the US-China trade war

Axel E. Rey

ISBN 9781692683238

About the Author

Axel Rey is a business economist providing macroeconomic and industrial consultancy services to corporate clients, he has worked for the past 22 years in the Greater China region of Hong Kong and mainland China.

Axel specializes in the area of gauging parametric values where the macroeconomic variables at issue are substantially pre-conditioned by institutional factors. Besides his multidisciplinary training in economics and commerce, he is among a handful of economists nowadays who are highly knowledgeable of the New Institutional Economics and applying this specialist knowledge to macroeconomic reasoning.

As a number of his former colleagues in Hong Kong he has befriended for decades are native speakers of the Chinese language, he is privileged by having access to a multitude of information sourced from China's high-finance sphere that are available only in the Chinese language, never previously made available to the English-speaking world.

The author can be contacted by   pro.public.interest@gmail.com

Preface

"No one knows who owes what to whom or how much, only when it starts to go bankrupt will things start falling apart."
- Peter Pauly, economics professor at the University of Toronto's Rotman School of Management. Commenting in 2018 on CNBC regarding China's shadow banking industry - likening it to scenarios seen before the 2007 US Subprime crisis.

This book reveals to the English-speaking world for the first time what Levin Y. Zhu, a top-echelon insider in China's high-finance sphere, has revealed about the actual debt level of China's - amounting to twice as big as the officially announced figure. Son of China's former Prime Minister Zhu Ronji, Levin Zhu is a former CEO to China International Capital Corporation (a state-owned investment bank joint-ventured with Morgan Stanley), had in 2018 estimated that the accruable total debt currently in China is, in reality, much larger than the generally acknowledged figure, of 300% of GDP. If the gargantuan amounts of debt carried by the shadow banking industry are included in the pile, Zhu estimated that the actual level of debt in China is about 600% of the country's 2018 GDP.

One will not be so astounded by said figure of 600%, if one also sees what Zhu has depicted in the context of macroeconomic sequencing, that is: in the China model of development, with each one trillion GDP created, comes along a 6 trillion of incremental debt.

With the on-going US-China trade war, we now live in a recalibrated global economy.

You may have read China's indebtedness problem covered by the press nowadays. However, reports done by mainstream media are often not much more than what's superficial and usually with a gloss-over of some sort at the end. An article titled, "Trade War With The U.S. Could Be The Tipping Point For China's $14 Trillion Debt-Ridden Economy", published by CNBC in April 2018.

Readers may get confused by such title, said US$14 Trillion is China's 2018 GDP, the debt load the nation carries now, using the figure conceded by Beijing's officials is at least 300% of that, which is, US$42.6 Trillion - about double in size to that same figure of the US (while China's economy is about 60% to that of the US). And, if we apply the aforesaid figure revealed by Levin Zhu, throwing in all the debts carried by the shadow banking industry, China's actual debts could be to the tune of US$85.2

Trillion.

The wording "tipping point" in that title seems revealing, but then the CNBC article also quotes from sources that give glossy euphemism to the situation, suggesting that the problems may likely be solved by further "reforms". Euphemistic 'explaining away' with all things that are China has been a typical practice by a majority of mainstream media in the U.S.

It is a known fact, that a host of mainstream U.S. media are now under heavy undue influence from certain business interests associated with those media, who in turn have earlier became vested interest entities affiliated to the propaganda machines in Beijing. As a result, ordinary investors nowadays could get hardly anything about China that's of much use, from most of the mainstream U.S. media reports and comments.

This book provides the reader with an opportunity to avoid being misled by all the now-abundant China-euphemist journalism. Besides intended euphemism, there are also plentiful misreading on reality about China in the west. This book enables the readers to better dispel both of the above. A majority of the information sources cited in this book were being made available to the English-speaking world for the first time.

Also, there are in abundance the China-euphemist westerner commentators in high-finance investment communities and some economic research establishments in making macroeconomic inferences. And these, are potentially detrimental to you the investor, with disinformation so created.

The case of China will demonstrate how China's peculiar Party-State institutional configuration plays a critical role in an untoward macroeconomic sequencing.

Content   (Book 1)

Appendix

For readers who have no knowledge in basic macroeconomics (or being 'rusty' in such knowledge). You Tube web links and illustrations for the macroeconomics concepts of multiplier effect and Propensity to Consume.

Chapter 1

An Economy Held Hostage

How all of China's 2017-18 economic growth were being 'written off' by the cost of interest servicing the nation's gargantuan debts

For the consecutive two years of 2017-18, *total interest costs in servicing China's gargantuan debt loads had much more than wiped out the entire gains from GDP growth.* Interest expenses required to service all the piles of debts in 2018 amount to 16% of China's GDP. That is, 1 in every 6 bucks created as the nation's output now needs to be expensed as the interest cost to carry the debt load that is now over 300% of the country's 2018 GDP.

Worse yet, China's *debts are now growing at a pace that's twice to the average rate of increase in debt worldwide.* And the problem is a structural one. This is because, in said over-300%-GDP debts, more than half of them are corporate debts, then two-thirds of that is with China's grossly inefficient and monopolistic State-owned Enterprise (SOE) sector.

That is, the SOEs' debt piles are now of the size of about 100% of China's 2018 GDP. And, in China's Party-State economic system all these SOEs do with their debts are just rolling over each year (get a new loan from the creditor, the State-owned banks, to cover principles of the loans plus unpaid interests from the previous year). This has been one of the main reasons for China's pace of debt increase double to that of the world average.

Also, what you don't see reported by mainstream media is that, China has now a foreign debt totaled to about US$2 Trillion, and with the RMB (China's currency) depreciating (mainly caused by the current trade-war situations), additional interest expenses are increasing owing to the exchange rate factor.

If we apply a principle in management accounting to China's GDP measurement, then *China's GDP growth rates for both of the two years of 2017 and 2018 are to be construed as negative.* Total interest expenses in servicing all the debts in China exceed the year's incremental GDP by US$ 712 billion and US$760 billion in 2017 and 2018 respectively, the latter figure (as depicted above), is 16% of China's 2018 GDP.

This gauge, of how incommensurate debt burdens have now more than offset the entire increments in output from China's GDP growth for the last 2 years, is very much an overlooked macroeconomic condition by economic researches on China the world over. And, this is also what Wall Street money managers and mainstream media will not want to tell you about, for reasons relating to their own vested interests.

Unreported in the west are Beijing's official figures for total interest expenses: In 2018, China's GDP has enlarged by circa US$1.38 Trillion but the total interest expenses paid to service all debts in the economy amount to about US$2.14 Trillion. And, the gap between the two, circa US$760 Billion, further widened from the same figure in 2017, of US$712 Billion.

Rating agency S&P assessed in September 2019 that, should the US-China trade war continue to escalate, China's GDP growth rate could decrease to 3.7% in worst scenarios for the next 10-year period. The S&P also gives an outlook of a protracted period of China's GDP growth downturn 10 years out.

- **Champion of growth, in debt, not GDP**

China is now the champion of growth, in debts and not in GDP. As mentioned, *the pace of debt increases now in China is twice to that of the world's average rate of growth in debt*. Since 2008, the rate of growth for increased indebtedness in China has been 12% on average, year after year.

That is, for the past decade, rate of increases in debts have always outpaced the GDP growth rate. People who are bullish about China's economy are perhaps all blindfolded about how a substantial portion of China's high GDP growth in the past decade were brought about by the illusionist ploys of debt-driven growth. And now is the advent of the pay-back time.

All of the above conditions are likely to worsen, as China's GDP growth is declining in the current economic downturn that many (such as those at aforesaid S&P research team) see for the next 10 years out - it is statistically proven now, corporate profitability has been declining across the board - and the on-going US-China trade war is likely to continue exacerbating the problems.

China's debt-to-GDP ratio has ballooned to more than 300% in 2018, from 160% a decade ago. Parallel to this, is what a Brookings Institute research has revealed, about the Incremental Capital-Output Ratio scenario, depicted by the researcher as metaphorically "a headwind three times as strong as it was ten years ago" (detailed in Chapter 4).

A snapshot for how disproportionate indebtedness is now seriously negating China's future economic growth potential: for the last 3 years alone, household debts have increased some 20 trillion RMB (China's currency), which is about 22.2% of the nation's 2018 GDP - more than 80% of that is for home buyer mortgages paying for the *hyperinflation in property prices*. Meanwhile, total consumption as an all-important element in GDP has in these 3 years decreased between 2 to 3 trillion RMB *year after year*. What was touted by Beijing, of making consumption the 'new engine of economic growth' now increasingly ring hollow.

To give a taste for said "hyperinflation in property price" situation: comparing property prices in Los Angeles and Shenzhen (one of the 4 megacities of China's), while the average salary in L.A. is around $60,000 per annum, for Shenzhen this figure is only $7,500. With Shenzhen's average household income being a mere 12.5% to that of L.A.'s, average residential property prices in Shenzhen ($805 per square foot) is currently about 127% to that of L.A.'s ($633 per square foot). That is, on average, **taking into consideration the average household incomes in the two cities, the average price-to-income ratio for residential property in Shenzhen is more than 10 times that of L.A.'s.**

A distortion to such scale warrants the author's calling it a *hyperinflation* in property prices. The terminology 'hyperinflation' is used to depict a rate of inflation that goes many folds for a comparably limited time span. With the aforesaid figures, of the average price-to-income ratios in the two cities in the US and China, for the past decade, this ratio had increased for more than 10 folds.

Such is an indicative figure for how China's home-buyer households (in hundreds of millions) are now heavily in debt, from their mortgage loans owing.

How much does this matter, to China's future economic growth potential? A majority of researches on China's economy has failed to identify this factor for its true pivotal importance, and you surely don't see this being reported by mainstream media in the US. This book shows you, how this urban property price hyperinflation has now transduced into one of the main elements causing (what we call in macroeconomics) the *multiplier effect* to shrink, and hence substantially negates the economy's future growth potential.

For the first time in 15 years, the sufficiency of China's Foreign Exchange Reserves is now in serious doubt, by the end of 2018, China's total foreign debts have reached a new height of US$ 1.965 Trillion. As an economy where exports and imports being pivotal to all economic activities, the significance in this is that an adequate foreign reserves level plays a critical role in maintaining macroeconomic stability and the efficacy in implementing monetary policies.

China's foreign debts have from 2017 to the first quarter of 2019 increased by a whopping 35%. The apparent book value of China's foreign exchange reserve that Beijing wants to show you, of (circa) US$ 3 trillion, is deceptive - it is not the *balance sheet* accrual value that you need to see. Chapter 7 of this book will show you how China's foreign reserves have now fallen to a rather inadequate level.

This book illustrates how China's economic future is beset by a range of institutionally-determined factors that caused such Great-Leap-Forward in debt-servicing costs - along with the followings: the phenomenal (hundreds of millions, of what's popularly dubbed in China as) "mortgage slave" households, and the myriads of corporate and government undertakings have led to a pattern of "Think-Big-turn-Sink-Big" undertakings pervading the economy. It shows how all these, in turn, necessitate the onset of a feedback looping between the *weakening macroeconomic multiplier effect* and *shriveling corporate profitability*. Then, how the US-China trade war is now enlarging these sinkholes in China's economy.

Note: For readers who have never studied the most basic course in economics, consult with this page's foot note. There is also a brief introduction to this multiplier effect concept in the book's Appendix.

- **Worse yet, what's with the gargantuan, forcefully self-serving SOE sector**

More structurally worrisome, is the fact that China's gargantuan and forcefully self-serving State-Owned Enterprise (SOE) sector now carried a debt load that is about the same size of the nation's 2018 GDP.

In April 2019, China's non-financial-institution corporate debts stand at about 153% of the 2018 GDP. An economist from a Chinese think tank reveals, about two-thirds

----

Multiplier effect, a quick explanation: An initial increase in spending, cycles recursively (person A's spending is person B's income, with this income person B will spend a percentage of it, and this spending becomes person C's income...) through the economy, resulting in incomes created that's multiple times larger than the initial dollar amount spent.

----

of this were incurred by State-owned Enterprises (SOEs), while around half of such

SOE debts relate to local government finance - this author: a majority of them are for white elephant public works for the boosting of local GDP, which in turn were so geared to actualize the local bureaucrat's individual gains in his career in the officialdom. These local white elephant public works give the economy a rate of zero, for their (analogically speaking) equivalent Return on Equity, in a social accounting perspective.

This depicts how grossly the SOEs have drained the nation's economic resources like a gargantuan sinkhole, how hugely they have created (what in standard Marshallian economic modeling illustrates as) social deadweight, and it is all necessitated by China's Party-state economic system. With the gargantuan and forcefully self-serving SOEs having monopolized the prerogative of low-interest rate loans from titanic state-owned banks - for an interest rate of circa 6%, in contrast to what the privately owned firms' financing costs, usually at interests of 12 to 20%.

Such inequitable advantages the SOEs command has transduced nothing to society's benefit, all there have been are aristocracy-like fat-cat party-cadre beneficent favored by this system of institutionalized cronyism. And, what you have learned from Economics 101 tells you, from the (key concept of) opportunity cost perspective, such an gargantuan, self-serving SOE sector impose gigantic opportunity costs to society. To wit, it is very much to society's detriment, in that the SOEs' corporate debts now is of such magnitude.

The China figure above is to be contrasted by the same US figure: Federal Reserve data shows, as of the end of 2018, the total non-financial institution corporate debt is about 73.9% of the U.S. GDP.

China's is an economy now held hostage, by a set of untoward macroeconomic sequencing necessitated by institutional predispositions intrinsic to the country's Party-State system. In 2018, the encapsulating concept pervading China's online forums about the state of the economy is "China's economy is now 'abducted' by the property market". This book illustrates how policymakers at Beijing's Party-State system have been risk-dyslexic in not having been cognizant of the grave dangers that have built up in the past decade as the economy went on a path of financialization.

- **Financialization of the economy - the China version**

The disproportionate indebtedness permeating the hundreds of millions of home-buyer households, corporate entities, and local governments were necessitated by an extreme type of financialization economy-wide, it is a pervasive supra-overdraft modality all across the broad, and it has prevailed for longer than the last decade. Then, its consequences have started to emerge since early 2018.

What took place in China's property markets needs to be characterized as the Financialization of Housing. Unbeknownst to and/or under-emphasized by most of those in the west conducting economic researches on China, is the fact that China is perhaps the only country on earth where residential property prices are *not included* as a factor in the nation's *consumer price index (CPI)*. As China's National Bureau of Statistics claims: residential properties are considered an item of "investment", and not "consumption".

This means the Chinese Communist Party (which determines everything that matters for any issue in China, certainly including how the CPI is compiled) has 'decreed' for the China-version of Financialization in property markets. This is an equivalent to, as if Beijing's National Bureau of Statistics (NBS) is treating all home-buyer households' accommodation arrangements with the condos they have bought and mortgaged to the banks, to be entirely free of charge. It illustrates, how arbitrary and untrustworthy the metric came out of the NBS can be.

'Illusionist' feats (what we depict a magician is doing on stage) *are one of the main features that characterize things that are China today.*

This book will demonstrate to you, what such China-version of financialization has brought in, the two transductions that shape the nation's macroeconomic future: (1) what is the earth-shaking macroeconomic implications stemming from the hyperinflation in urban property prices and gargantuan buildups of property gluts. (2) how the prevalence of the China-version financialization has coagulate-cascaded into a dominant modulation of adverse-selection in China's corporate sphere.

China is a place where the Party-State system does not recognize an array of things that are considered universal values or norms around the world. The aforesaid CPI computation, which excludes the residential property price as a factor, signifies the surreally distorted market mechanism in China's property sector.

This Financialization of Housing portraits for an extremity in the nation's financialization of the economy. It is evidenced by the fact that, in recent years, about one-third of China's GDP was created by the urban property sector alone. With such 'mirage valuation' modality in China's property market, by which condo-buyer households typically spend more than half of their monthly disposable income (usually *much* more than half), to service their mortgage loans, it is having *most* (if not all) of their discretionary consumption stripped away from them (hence the popular dubbing used in China, of the "mortgage slave" phenomenon).

Total mortgage loans issued in China were at the end of 2018, about more than three times to that of the entire banking system's lending to all manufacturing industries in the country. For an economy having evolved as one that is geared to manufacturing and exporting, in how economic growth potential is to be sustained, said figure signifies a grave misallocation of resources with inescapable macroeconomic consequences.

For just the 3 years to end of 2018, China's *household indebtedness has increased by* about *22.2% of the nation's 2018 GDP* while the **consumption element in the GDP equation has decreased** by some 3.3% of the country's 2018 GDP. Percentage-wise it may not seem big, but the importance in this, is that it signifies the *reversal of a secular trend* China's economy has had for decades - of an on-average steady growth of the consumption component in the GDP equation. And this, the increase in the consumption weighting in GDP, is much needed especially for the current stage of the economy, where all other already overstretched engines of growth now turn increasingly ineffective, fast. This book will demonstrate in its following chapters, how said reversal signals for the start of a *downturn in the consumption component of GDP* like never before.

Incommensurate household indebtedness will conjunct incommensurate corporate indebtedness through the macroeconomic circular flow. A telling profiling for China's corporate indebtedness can be evinced by the following figure:

The Evergrande Group, one of China's top-three property developers, has in April 2019 issued US$700 million corporate bond overseas at a junk-bond coupon rate of 10.5%. Much of the proceeds from that issuance is to pay for the interest expense of the firm's existing debts. This implicates how intrinsically insolvent the firm's state of finance is, the one firm has now an outstanding debt of US$ 113.7 billion, about half of that amount will fall due in the next 10 months while 75% of the total corporate debt will fall due in the next 2 years. The firm is now offering a desperate 40% discount to promote sales in its properties unsold nation-wide, in the midst of the huge property gluts all around China. Unoccupied properties nation-wide in medium and large cities is now on average 22.2%, for the largest 4 cities it is 16.8%.

One other chunk of corporate debts is serviced by China's estimated US$20 trillion shadow banking industry. Reported in 2018 by CNBC, quoting Peter Pauly, an economics professor at Toronto's Rotman School of Management, for his assessment of China's Shadow banking industry: "China's underdeveloped banking sector with little regulation, ...Its US$20 trillion shadow banking industry, which is nearly impossible to figure out. In fact, the value of nonperforming loans could get even worse, if only people knew just what was happening inside of this murky shadow banking sector."

The report went on: "China's shadow banking system may be the most worrisome financial issue in decades, even more problematic than the sub-prime mortgage meltdown that fueled America's financial crisis." Then Pauly made the striking depiction: "No one knows who owes what to whom or how much," said Pauly. "Only when it starts to go bankrupt will things start falling apart."

- **China is much more reliant on exports for its growth, than what you see from the superficial export-to-GDP figure**

As mentioned earlier, rating agency S&P assessed in September 2019 that, should the US-China trade war continue to escalate, China's GDP growth rate could decrease to as low as 3.7% in the worst scenario.

Importantly, the part of the incomes in GDP created by exports has much higher macroeconomic multiplier value than are GDP created by domestic transactions owing to China's overly high sales taxes and other leakages in the macroeconomic circular flow. An extreme case of the high sales taxes is, if you buy a personal computer in China, nearly half of the purchase price goes to pay for the taxes.

This means, there is a double whammy in the reduction from net exports: decreases in net exports will not only make the size of the net-export element in the GDP equation to decrease, it will also make the economy-wide multiplier effect to shrink. Researches on China's economy around the world, including those that were done by Beijing's policymaker think-tank instrumentalities, have generally failed to recognize this important aspect, of how much exports matters to China's macroeconomic viability. *Note: readers who are not familiar with the basic macroeconomic descriptions above may consult with the Appendix at the end of this book.*

We are now in a new era of world trade, characterized by the readiness and continuation of the US and EU reprisals to Beijing's failing to honor its promises, of transforming its economic system towards a more equitable market system that warrants the entitlement of low tariff - the privilege assigned by its WTO membership. Having exceeded the 15-year mark from the time China was admitted into the WTO, the day of reckoning has come in Q2 2018.

How much does the trade war impact on China's economy? The manufacturing sector geared to exporting accounts for about 30% of China's employment, while all jobs linked to exports consists circa 40% of all employment in the nation. With just an increase in tariff to 10% for the US$ 50 billion worth of goods the US imports from China started from late 2018, there has already been a decrease of 30% in such imports by April 2019. May 10th 2019 is when tariff goes up to 25% with the further US$ 200 billion, and a 10-25% of tariff will at a later stage be applied to a further US$325 billion worth of China's exports to the US. How much does US imports count as weight in all of China's exports? The following facts are eye-opening: *in 2018, around 90% of China's (circa US$ 350 billion) trade surplus earnings from exports to the world was garnered from its exports to the US alone* - even though only 20% of all of China's exports (by value) were sold to the US.

This is how pivotal the US market is to China, with the following specifics:

1. Even as total exports consist 18.24% of China's GDP (2018), it is estimated that some 400 million employments in China (a lot more than half of all its urban jobs) are directly or indirectly linked to its export industries. And, as aforementioned, the US market is where 90% of all of China's trade surplus earnings were garnered.

2. The above figure of 18.24% is highly delusive, as big chunks of China's GDP have in recent years been generated by transactions with the *ultra-valuation modality in the property market, which in the last 3 years account for about one-third of China's GDP.* Such non-sustainable GDP creation modality owing to hyperinflation in property prices has *diluted the genuine weight of the total export in China's GDP.*

And, together with the part of the GDP created by all of those local government white-elephant public works, these two GDP-boosters are the abnormalities and for a really sensible statistical treatment to account for a secular trend going forward, we will need to deflate what the hyper-inflated property prices and profligate public works have rendered as China's GDP figures in past years. If we retro-fit the GDP weightings, taking into due consideration for what ought to look like, by deflate the weightings with said two chunks of anomaly GDP creations, the export sector's share in China's GDP would be much higher - under such adjusting for a more genuine GDP composition, the export sector's weight in China's GDP could easily be above 35%.

3. Higher level of net export (total exports minus total imports) means lower

propensity to import, hence it also make the macroeconomic *multiplier value* to go higher, as foreign consumers' purchase is a macroeconomic equivalent to an increase in domestic consumption. That means, lower level of exports to the US will make China's macroeconomic multiplier value to shrink.

4. There is also a qualitative, or parametric, prognosis needed, regarding the aforesaid two chunks of GDP created by the property sector and the white-elephant public works, as mainstay GDP boosters: they generate disproportionately fewer jobs and these employments being unsustainable in nature. This need to be looked at side by side with what the gargantuan, forcefully self-serving SOEs' virtually zero job creation - with their myriads of negative return-to-equity ratio projects.

5. The prospect of a 25% tariff for goods made in China entering the US market has expedited the further extractions of entire supply chains for an overwhelming majority of manufacturing industries from China.

6. Out of the 10 largest firms that account for China's exports, 8 of them are tech-sector companies from Taiwan (which is not under China's control, economically, and politically), and their mainstay exports are to the US. The 25% tariff have already caused all these firms to moving their manufacturing base back to Taiwan, or elsewhere out of China. This is especially the case with the prospect of a Free Trade Agreement between Taiwan and the U.S. For the last 20 years you can scarcely see any product you buy that says "Made in Taiwan", because a huge number of products that say "Made in China" were made by companies from Taiwan manufacturing in China. This is going to change from now on.

7. Economic analysis has estimated that, China will bear 20.5% of the burden in that 25% of the tariff, while only 4.5% will be borne by entities at the US end.

Chapter 2

How China's debt-driven growth model has the entire world fooled

6 trillion debt is required for the creation of 1 trillion GDP

Levin Y. Zhu, a former CEO to China International Capital Corporation (Beijing's own investment bank, a joint-venture with Morgan Stanley) had in 2018 estimated that the accrued total debt currently in China is actually much larger than that of 300% of GDP, as colossal amounts of debts, carried in the shadow banking industry is not being included in the pile. To make sense of the scale, total profits made by all listed companies in China in 2017 was a mere 3.7% of China's 2018 GDP. Notice that this figure of 2017 was attained prior to the onset of the trade war effects started in early 2018.

Zhu further revealed in 2018 that *in the China model of development, with each one trillion GDP created, comes along a 6 trillion of incremental debt.*

This greatly helped to explain for the phenomenal Great-Leap-Forward of China's indebtedness in recent years, that China's debt-to-GDP ratio has ballooned to more than 300 percent from 160 percent a decade ago. The pace of debt increases now in China is double to such rate on average world-wide. Since 2008, the rate of growth for increased indebtedness in China has been 12% on average, year after year.

The "six-trillion debt for one-trillion GDP" prognosis is manifestation of (what this author characterizes as) China's *institutional dyspraxia* of its Party-State system. There are the macroeconomic conditions predisposed by institutionally-determined factors in two broad categories:

(1) *A 'pandemic-scale' misallocation of economic resources* with (what this author characterizes as) a *corporate caste system*: the gargantuan and forcefully self-serving state-owned enterprises (SOEs) sector and the ensemble monopolistic deadweight created by this and all the special-interest entities owned by Communist Party

princeling cadres (such as the arbitrary toll booth settings on all of China's superhighways).

(2) **_The shrinking macroeconomic multiplier effect_** that fundamentally negates future growth potentials. And this is necessitated by:

(a) a "mortgage serfdom" economy,

(b) the logistics cost in general that's much higher than all other major economies in the world owing to the special-interest entities mentioned in (1) above,

(c) a disproportionately-high sales tax regime, and

(d) (what this author characterizes as) a *'financial caste system'*: while privately-owned firms generate over 70% of the nation's urban employment, they generally do not bet loans from state-owned banks and need to pay very high rate of interest to borrow for their business undertakings, to the tune of 12% - 20%

As the 2018 statistics shows, privately-owned companies' profit on average has decreased by 26%, foreign-owned, decrease on average by 9%. But SOEs had on average an increase of profit by 9%. You can be assured that this SOE profitability figure comes from the inglorious monopolistic powers that they hold, and in no way from efficiency or anything that's socially desirable (such as innovation). It simply demonstrates how China's Party-State economic system has in it the domineering of a most inequitable modulation running in the economy. Privately-owned firms generate over 70% of all the urban-area jobs in China, while the SOEs monopolize over two-thirds of all the nation's resources.

A best example to this is, China Southern Airline, one of the major-league SOEs, was making lucrative profits by re-lending the funds it borrowed from state-owned banks at low interest rates to privately owned small and medium-sized firms, charging very high interests - for much of the last decade. To see the scale of the exploitation in this, the banks will pay around 3% interest for its clients' savings account and privately owned businesses, with an absolute majority in them unable to borrow from state-owned banks, are borrowing at an interest of 12% to 20% from roundabout channels such as the shadow banking system.

For sure there are numerous other SOEs that have practiced for longer than the last decade, profiting from this kind of 'perfectly legal' Loan-Shark business. Perhaps an illustrative dubbing for this would be: a financial caste system. In China, people in the streets would tell you they see things like this no different from many other government decrees.

In China, it is altogether rare for any privately-owned firms being capable of getting approved of any loan from the titans of state-owned banks. And, privately-owned banks in China have only a very small market share in China's banking industry. Interest rates in the non-bank lending sphere (or, shadow banking), likely at the going rate of 12% - 20%. And that's how most privately-owned firms get their finance from - while privately-owned firms actually provide more than 70% of urban employment across China.

This brought in a deleterious macroeconomic consequence. In our peculiar case of China, the SOEs get their loans from state-owned banks at the low interest rates such as 5% - 6%, while (as mentioned) privately-owned firms generally need to pay very high rate of interest to borrow for their business undertakings, to the tune of 12% - 20%, such institutional peculiarity (this author dubs, a financial caste system) *shrinks the economy-wide macroeconomic multiplier effect.*

The forcefully self-serving presence of the SOEs, extracting monopolistic profits from society gobbling up with all the undue prerogatives they hold, is in practice a *corporate and financial caste system,* it *fundamentally misallocates resources economy-wide.* China's is a system akin to what's being called (in economic history) mercantilism. And, compared to the mercantilist system in 18th-century Europe, the China version today features grossly lower efficiency - as the China version is predicated on a far less equitable institutional setting, and hence the working of price mechanism is much more impaired.

From a standard Marshallian perspective in economics, we say such system carries enormous social deadweight. Instances aforementioned depict for how inefficient and inequitable China's Party-State economic system is. China's SOEs need to be visualized by the economic theory of externality, analogical to what happens when certain productions generate tremendous pollution and the social costs incurred therein were burdened to society as a whole, instead of the polluters getting taxed and therefore such externality being internalized/redressed. In China's Party-State system, the way China's SOEs are operated give out what we call "negative externalities" in economics, to society as a whole.

- **Visualizing China's mercantilist statecraft**

Ivory-tower economists around the world have generally failed to identify China's economy in a taxonomy that more sensibly maps the diverse economic systems.

China is a mercantilist economic system. We need such signpost "mercantilism" - in differentiating a mercantilist system from a genuine market-based economic system (or, in the less rigorous, colloquial terms, capitalist economic system), it importantly makes sense of how China's debt-driven growth model came about.

Mercantilism, the economic system practiced in antiquity Europe before the genuine market-based economic system came into being. In a mercantilist system, the statecraft, entirely controlled by the ruling aristocracy, implements predatory commerce: (1), to empower the development of domestic manufacturing without the ordinary workers' share in GDP grow proportionately to productivity gains economy-wide, and (2), to pursue international trade not based on the (Ricardian) principle of comparative advantages, but on a predatory rationale.

An illustrative instance is given by the global steel industry. Cost advantages gained by violating the WTO rules (of equitable labor, environmental, and non-subsidy considerations) have rendered China's cost structure in the steel industry gaining substantial competitive edge - then relevant WTO rules being unenforceable with an effective mechanism to retard such violation. Then Beijing has been more than ready to pursue its predatory mercantilist policy: dumping in international trade to drive steel manufacturers in the developed world out of business, to push forward its monopolistic objectives. Nothing substantial was being done about this until the onset of the US-China trade war started Q2 2018.

What is in the case of China since 1979, is nothing much more than replacing the aristocracy in the antiquity Europe with China's Party-state masters, for who solely controls the statecraft.

In European economic history, with the constant enlarging of the middle class and advancements in the democratic, rule-of-law social governance, the mercantilist economic system of antiquity Europe had eventually evolved into the genuine market-based economic system (where nothing is 'not subject to the discipline of the market').

For China, the Party-State system certainly does not allow any bit of anything that can be called the advancement in democratic, rule-of-law socio-economic governance. This is the institutional predisposition that negates the debt-driven development model to take shape in any way resembling the case of South Korea illustrated earlier. Worse yet, hyperinflation in property prices has now rendered the downgrading of consumption statistically seen in 2017-18, with perhaps three-quarter of the supposed-to-be middle-class home-buyer households.

Only when one visualizes in such 'augmented reality', one is enabled in making sense of how a *Faustian sequencing* for the decades of *'creation of GDP for the sake of creating GDP'* type of policy mindset. That is, such mindset being permissive to firstly, the gigantic chunks in the economy that are *'not subject to the discipline of the market'*: the gargantuan and forcefully self-serving State-owned Enterprise (SOE) sector's overcapacity buildups and the local governments' white-elephant public work and 'ghost industrial park' buildups in past decades; and then secondly, being permissive to the hyperinflation in urban property prices, which resulted in the property development sector being (for an extended period of time) *'exempt' from the discipline of the market*. This is evidenced by the currently circa 22% unsold and vacant urban properties - included in these are the hundreds of 'ghost cities' now in China.

All these *'not subject to the discipline of the market'* and *'exempt' from the discipline of the market (for the time being)* buildups created enormous GDP for decades. But it is a *Faustian sequencing*, and the day of reckoning has come - we now see China's interest expenses to service its gargantuan debts have much more than wiped out all of the economy's 2017-18 GDP growth increments, and this come with dire consequences in terms of how it weakens the all-important multiplier effect, the key element in macroeconomic sequencing that determines the economy's future growth potential. This will be illuminated in following chapters.

On the international trade front, the day of reckoning for Beijing's mercantilist practices has also arrived in Q2 2018, the start of the US-China trade war.

- **Two decades of "creation of GDP for the sake of creating GDP"**

To gauge China's future economic potential, one has o first come to a panoramic view about the insidious nature in local government spending through longer than the past decade - having in it the mindset of "creation of GDP (solely) for the sake of creating GDP". That is, in China's Party-State system, arguably some 75% of all the public works are of the White-Elephant nature. Behind all this is the incentive in serving the local bureaucrats' individual gains. That is, the local officials' promotions, or at least staying put, are hinged upon the GDP created in the year, set as the number-one metric for job performance. Alongside this is the local governments' typical financing undertaking, in monetizing state lands - the collusive profiteering together with property developers that have eventuated in the gargantuan amounts built, of empty urban condos, ghost cities, and ghost industrial parks. The macroeconomic consequence necessitated by such a plethora of profligacy is now a centrality theme - what this author will demonstrate as a key causation for the *dwindling* of what we call the *multiplier effect* in macroeconomics.

Corporate debt to GDP is a key indicator for the economy's growth potential. There are less than a dozen countries in the developed world having corporate-debt-to-GDP ratios that are above the 110% mark. What's unique about China's figure, of 153%, is not that it's *quantitatively* among the highest ones, but that none other in the world has a *qualitatively* egregious profiling with its corporate debts. That is, in China's unique Party-State system, a substantial portion of the corporate debts were incurred by reckless expansionism enabled by a system of financial cronyism.

In such a system, there is the predominance of what's called the *adverse selection* in the specialized field of information economics. This is attributable to the fact that the gargantuan, self-serving SOEs are entitled to operate in ways that are virtually **not subject to the discipline of the market.** The scale of deficiencies entailed from such a *corporate caste system* is sufficient in constituting what we call in classical economic theory the *social deadweight,* in gargantuan magnitudes. As this book will demonstrate, how such colossal *social deadweight* come to substantially negate future economic growth potentials of the nation.

Beijing's expediency-driven system of mercantilism and debt-driven growth module that seems to have brought desired results to the economy in the past two decades has now inescapably entered into a phase of backlashes necessitated by the inbuilt instructional deficiencies. Intrinsic to the presence of omnipotent vested interest groups is (what this author dubs) the *institutional dyspraxia* in the country's Party-State economic system.

By not being knowledgeable of what's *inbuilt in China's institutional predispositions*, the ivory-tower economists around the world have not been able to come to grip with an array of inherent predicaments underlying the country's economy.

Reported on Oct. 16 2018 by CNBC was S&P's assessment on China's local government debts: "The actual level of off-balance-sheet Chinese local government debt could be several times more than what is publicly disclosed, (to be as high as) US$5.78 trillion". This figure is close to 50% of China's 2018 GDP. And, with the report quoted, the S&P analyst's metaphor of "That's a debt iceberg with titanic credit risks", one needs to go much beyond such journalistic portrait to visualize the true underlying mechanism at work - what this author called *institutional dyspraxia*.

There have been in abundance the China-euphemist westerner commentators in the investment consulting communities, helping to propagate the neglecting of pivotal facts in critical junctures when making macroeconomic inferences. Investors under such undue influences are subject to nasty surprises down the road. In June 2017, Goldman Sachs' CEO posted on Goldman's website a 3-minute video clip "China: Confidence on the Rise". How easy it is, for crucial macroeconomic profiling to be entirely neglected by major-league players on Wall Street. What some money managers wouldn't do just to advance their personal gains? Your rights, in knowing what the facts are about China, were being deprived.

People around the world have in the past decade been misled by the plentiful of China-Euphemist media and Wall Street investment bankers acted as self-serving cronies of Beijing's, propagating disinformation for their own gains. This book will demonstrate to you solid evidence - many of them were never being made available to the English-speaking world before.

There have been in abundance the China-euphemist westerner commentators in the investment consulting communities, helping to propagate the neglecting of pivotal facts in critical junctures when making macroeconomic inferences. Investors under such undue influences are subject to nasty surprises down the road. In June 2017, Goldman Sachs' CEO posted on Goldman's website a 3-minute video clip "China: Confidence on the Rise". How easy it is, for crucial macroeconomic profiling to be entirely neglected by major-league players on Wall Street. What some money managers wouldn't do just to advance their personal gains? Your rights, in knowing what the facts are about China, were being deprived.

People around the world have in the past decade been grossly misled by the plentiful of China-Euphemist media and Wall Street investment bankers acted as self-serving cronies of Beijing's, propagating disinformation for their own gains. This book will demonstrate to you solid evidence - many of them were never being made available to the English-speaking world before.

- **One in every 6 bucks created as the nation's GDP is expensed outright, for overdrafts expended earlier**

At an average interest rate of 7.6%, China's 2018 debt-servicing interest cost is circa RMB 14.4 Trillion. That is, about 16% of the GDP created were, *in effect, written off as expenses* just to service all the debts incurred from before. This amount much exceeds the year's increment to the total GDP, of RMB 9.3 Trillion. And, the gap between the two, RMB 5.1 Trillion, has widened from what was in 2017, which is RMB 4.8 Trillion.

This widening gap indicates two important attributes in China's economic system:

First, a substantial portion of the debts were generated by the rollover loans from previous debts. That is, as the debtor corporate entity was not able to repay at the due day, it managed to borrow a (bigger) new loan to pay back the old loan plus interests owing. Such is a common practice between China's state-owned banks and state-owned enterprises, a thing characteristic of China's Party-State system. Potentially a perilous snow-balling.

Secondly, ultra-high property valuation for the last decade was further accelerated during the last 3 years thanks to, among other things, an improvisation called "Penggai", that made property prices in smaller (called the in China the 3rd and 4th tier) cities to soar to unrealistic highs (this will be explained in a latter chapter). At the end of 2018, total mortgage loans plus other types of household debts that were also widely used for condo-buying amounts to 3 times that of the total lending from China's banking system to all manufacturing industries. And you will see why this feature in bank lending is deleterious a thing later in this book.

The macroeconomic significance in this is, such heavy indebtedness is now enlarging a *sinkhole*, that is: any incremental portion of the GDP no longer generates what is in macroeconomics called the multiplier effect, which is key to a 'healthy' macroeconomic state of affairs. And this, given a number of other factors on-going in China's economy, is of grave consequences. In the jargon of macroeconomics, consumer confidence determines the size of *Marginal Propensity to Consume* (MPC) and hence the magnitude of the multiplier effect. In this perspective, things in China have now demonstrated for the start of an era where the economy is chugging along with an increasingly 'impaired' multiplier effect. That is, disproportionate indebtedness necessarily negates the magnitude of two linchpin components in our GDP equation: the MPC, and corporate investments. And hence, disproportionate indebtedness substantially weakens the multiplier effect. For those who have gained knowledge from economics 101, you would be able to see how said debt burden to such scale will, through macroeconomic circular flow, cause the repercussion in the increase in unemployment.

More bad news is to be seen: it is now estimated by reportedly credible sources that China is now also carrying a foreign debt load of about US$ 1.9 trillion. As RMB (China's currency) has underwent sizable depreciation in 2019, the debt-servicing interest costs toward these foreign debts are increasing.

A consensus among many of China's own economic researches indicates that for every one percentage point drop in China's GDP growth rate, there will be somewhat an 8-million job loss in the economy.

This author will demonstrate to you how the fact that China's debt-servicing interest costs, now consume much more than the entire annual GDP growth, together with the on-going US-China trade war, have provided sufficient conditions capable of instating a deleterious feedback loop, rendering Beijing's monetary and fiscal stimulus measures increasingly ineffective, and brought in tidal waves of unemployment forthcoming.

This author points out the centrality in such weakening of the multiplier effect, in gauging China's economic future. And requisite analyses in this particular point is almost altogether amiss among existing economic researches on China.

- **The centrality of multiplier effect**

To detailing what we have elicited in a previous section, in our peculiar case of China, mainly 4 categories of institutionally-determined factors are inescapably bringing down the value of the nation's macroeconomic multiplier, and hence the economy's future growth potential:

(1). Hyperinflation in property prices lowers household *Marginal Propensity to Consume* (MPC) and hence short-change the household part of the *multiplier effect* economy-wide. This will be elaborated in chapters that follow.

(2). The *financial caste system:* The SOEs get their loans from state-owned banks at the low-interest rates such as 5% - 6%, while privately-owned firms create more than 70% of all the urban jobs in China, the absolute majority of privately-owned firms generally don't get their loans from state-owned banks and need to pay very high rate of interest to borrow for their business undertakings, to the tune of 12% - 20%. This institutional factor brought in the macroeconomic consequence of as it causes a larger overall mark-up in price with goods and services and may also at the same time thinning profitability in the private sector, it shrinks the economy-wide macroeconomic multiplier effect.

(3) The *corporate caste system*: Low efficiency and arbitrary market power in pricing are characteristic of all SOEs and the communist-party-princeling-owned monopolistic business entities. The most egregious case in this being: logistics cost amounts to 18% of China's GDP- one of the major factors that made consumer goods prices unreasonably much higher than they otherwise would be. Logistics costs (warehousing and transporting of goods) comprise 18% of China's GDP. By contrast, among the three largest economies in the world, Japan's logistics costs comprise

only 8% of GDP, and for the US, this figure is 9%. A big chunk in that obscenely high logistics costs is attributable to the fact that in China, superhighways have their highway tolls not collected by local governments, the managing of the roads was contracted out to companies owned by the princeling cadres (descendants of prominent and influential senior communist officials).

Likewise, This institutional factor causes a larger overall mark-up in price with consumer goods and services in general, and may at the same time thinning profitability in the private sector. Thus it shrinks the economy-wide macroeconomic multiplier effect.

(4) Sales taxes and tariffs for imports are generally much higher in China than in any other major economies in the world, the extreme case in this is that if you buy a notebook (or laptop) computer in China, about half of the purchase price you paid goes to sale taxes.

It is known in macroeconomics that the multiplier value becomes lower when:
- Propensity to consume is lower - high consumer debts suffice this condition. In the current China case, much more than half of ordinary home-buyer consumer households' dispensable income are used for mortgage payment, this significantly lowers home-buyer households' (in hundreds of millions) propensity to consume
- When there are non-price causes for net exports to decrease, such as what is now in the US-China trade war
- Taxes are higher
- Corporate profitability impaired by high corporate debts and high interest expenses for business loans - both being the case for China: (1) the SOEs debts is now about 100% of China's 2018 GDP, (2) for all the privately-owned firms that creates more than 70% of urban jobs, the prevailing interest rate for business loans is debilitating - 12% to 20%.

In short, with its mercantilist, Party-State system, China has for longer than a decade pursued debt-driven growth, and by doing so it has managed to have the entire world fooled (in having mistakenly perceived China's high GDP growth as a path of development repeating what we saw of the cases of South Korea and Taiwan in the 1970s and 1980s). Then the day of reckoning has now come, to such Faustian macroeconomic sequencing.

China's institutional predispositions simply suffice all of the traits listed above, for getting slapped all of the disorder diagnoses there, for the macroeconomic multiplier effect to go on shrinking.

Note: this author is fond of borrowing terminologies from biological and medical terms in depicting economic situations. He follows what Alfred Marshall, who laid the foundation for what we have today as the mathematical models in microeconomics, is known to have used repeated invocation of biological analogies in many of his seminal works. "Alfred Marshall points out that biology is natural economics" (Ghiselin, 1978)

Besides the above list of factors, China's institutionally-determined inefficiency that has caused an extraordinarily high logistics cost, amounting to 18% of the GDP, means consumer goods are disproportionately high in price as is compared to ordinary household income, this by itself also feeds into what's in the first item of the list - lower propensity to consume.

Chapter 3

Walking the tightrope of a Tri-lemma

Hefty indebtedness, dwindling corporate profitability, and the downgrading of middle-class consumption

Debts are not necessarily perilous a thing if the prospect of profitability with the majority of companies in the economy being reasonably promising, and, in such case corporate leveraging (debt-incurring) activities feeds into the augmenting of macroeconomic multiplier effect. South Korea provides a case in economic history, of a nation that's hefty in debt for decades, but then built up a competitive base in the era of globalized manufacturing and emerged triumphant with conducive corporate profitability and a multiplier effect scenario that conjunct an enlarging middle class. For our China case on hand, said South Korean model is not what has been happening, with its reigning Party-State economic system.

Institutional configurations make the fundamental difference between the two cases. In the South Korean case, nothing in the economy is *'not subject to the discipline of the market'* - like what's with the swelling State-owned Enterprises (SOEs) in China. On the other hand, as what aforesaid high-profile insiders like Zhu and Xiang (quoted earlier) have pointed to, there is pervading the corporate and local government sectors *the domineering of an insidious modulation for blind expansionism*, financed by state-owned banks (with these banks' being also in some critical junctures *'not subject to the discipline of the market'*). Local government financing for superfluous projects have also been much linked to the banks' off-the-balance-sheet shadow-banking ploys.

For longer than a decade, local governments and State-Owned corporations in China have through debt financing pumped out what this author dubs *a 'New Chinese Great Wall' scale of infrastructure buildups* and Soviet-style expansion in heavy industries - with substantial portions in them being white-elephant public works and big sunk-cost overcapacity that incur enormous 'opportunity costs' (what you have learned in economics 101) and *may prove next-to-nothing in lifting the overall productivity in the economy.* Instances like the dazzling buildups of China's high-speed rail network is a manifestation of a general pattern of *inbuilt insolvent proclivity* with these contrivances.

The attested revenue records from China's high-speed rail operation in years tells you that the entire planning for this herculean enterprise was never subject to the scrutiny, using commercially viable parameters. This is one more instance demonstrating what China's pseudo-market, the system may incur as Think-Big-turn-Sink-Big consequences. In this Party-State mercantilist system, the state-owned heavy-weights in the economy is run in ways that are *'not subject to the discipline of the market'* - hence there is the inescapable, inbuilt insolvent proclivity pervading in multiple facets of the economy.

- **The "Sink-Big" problems in China's high-speed rail system and local government white-elephant infrastructure buildups**

While the building of some 20,000 Kilometers of high-speed rail had also substantially helped boost China's GDP in the last decade, now the State Railway Corporation is RMB 5.28 Trillion in debt (i.e., this *one* State-owned enterprise (SOE) now carries a debt load that's nearly 6% of the country's 2018 GDP), while the *annual revenue of the high-speed rail operation is a mere RMB 340 billion,* which is some RMB 20 billion short of the annual *interest cost, of RMB 360 billion*, just to service that debt pile of RMB 5.28 Trillion. Out of all the high-speed rail routes, there is the *only route* (Beijing to Shanghai) being rather marginally profitable with every other routes continued in a money-losing state.

Not only that, the expansion of high-speed railways with its hefty indebtedness incurred and comparably paltry revenue generated has, in actuality, significantly pushed up logistics (cargo transportation) costs in China. Zhao Jian, an economics professor at Beijing University of Transportation (Beijing Jiaotong University, one of the best engineering university in China) has published 2 articles on Caixing Weekly, a leading online business newspaper in China. The articles points out, as the high-speed rail being exclusively a passenger carrier, the extensive uses of high-speed rail have resulted in a significant crowding-out effect. That is, big-ticket investments on high-speed rails take away funds that can otherwise (needed to) be invested to rationalize and improve the cargo transport portion of the railway system nation-wide. And, this has in actuality caused structural degradation in the cargo transport part of the nation-wide railway system and hence decreased efficiency in relevant resources allocation, then it has already caused prices with China's logistic costs to have increased substantially.

Such is an ominous case in what we call in economics the crowding-out effect from big-ticket fiscal expenditure. This means, the Herculean contrivance in China's high-speed rails now end up one more factor that elicit the pro-cyclical effect towards the current recessionary state of the economy. And that may contribute towards a probable worse-scenario for China's economic cycle to veer into a phase known as (the worst-possible macroeconomic scenario of) stagflation - the building and operation of China's high-speed rail system ends up becoming a model recipe, contributing to the forming of a stagflation state of the economy: hefty indebtedness linked to large fiscal spending that have helped depleting the government's coffer and hence reduced the room for counter-cyclical fiscal measures. Then in the current recessionary conditions, what comes out of the big-ticket public-work investment, of this high speed rail system, not only have failed to lift productivity related to the logistic side, it caused large increases in the logistic cost for goods transportation, which poses inflationary pressure.

China is known to have an extraordinarily inefficient logistics system even before the extensive high-speed railways was built, owing to institutionally determined factors such as the overcharging superhighway tolls (all superhighways are contracted to companies owned by the top Communist Party princeling cadres for them to set arbitrary toll booths, some as dense as 20 kilometers apart) and other administrative and monopolistic charges related to tracking. This is reflected by the fact that logistic costs (transportation and warehousing) amount to about 18% of China's GDP, in contrast to the 9% and 8% for the same figures in the US and Japan respectively.

Now with the extensive high-speed rail built and the aforesaid crowding-out effect and degrading of the railways' cargo transport functionality, the logistical cost cannot but go further higher. All these heightened costs for shipping the goods are equivalent to a poll tax on every consumer, and this has in it the effect of shrinking the all-important macroeconomic multiplier articulated earlier. In short, the economic detriments resulting from the building of extensive high-speed railways do not stop at those dimensions aforementioned from said transportation economist of said specialist university in Beijing, it also has the effect in contributing to the shrinking of the macroeconomic multiplier and hence have become one additional factor that negates China's future growth potential.

Across the nation, there have been for decades the thousands of big-ticket white-elephant public works built by local governments for two purposes:

One, to boost the local GDP figure (such that the local bureaucrat gets promoted, or at least hold on to their posts) but all these have now made local governments steeped in debts. And two, to create opportunities for the local bureaucrats to embezzle funds from the public work projects.

That tells you, how might certain types of self-serving plus corruptive purposes in the officialdom have been in reality a significant factor that boosted China's past economic growth figures at enormous costs to the nation's economic future. A public work expenditure did create the GDP of that year, but it also did *undermine the economy's long-run growth potential* as all the white-elephant public works *incur colossal debts but do not lift the economy's productivity.*

An array of cumulative causations that have led to China's current indebtedness is now exacerbated by the on-going US-China trade war, with which, China's gain from exports will be severely undermined. Millions of jobs have already been lost in 2018 and the first half of 2019, and more are at risk going forward.

Researches show that circa 40% of all the jobs in China are linked to exports. The spiraling-up costs the manufacturing industry faces in recent years, plus the US-China trade war since Q2 2018 have, now already caused more than half of all the foreign firms in the supply-chains with numerous manufacturing industries to exit China and moved elsewhere.

The impact of these exoduses has already caused huge unemployment. The official statement (likely underestimated) for 2018 reported 7.4 million laborers working in the urban manufacturing and construction sectors have lost their jobs and returned to their rural homes. Typical of how Beijing's propaganda machine would convey the aforesaid statistics, it has pronounced that in 2018, 7.4 million workers have returned to their rural home towns "to start new businesses" - well you know what it means if you are quite knowledgeable about how things are being run in China.

Already in 2017, The International Monetary Fund has warned that "China's reliance on debts - funded through an 'increasingly opaque and complex financial system' - to drive growth will eventually raise the specter of a 'disruptive' correction in growth in the longer term." And, given the omnipotent vested interest group in the Party-State system, there has been nothing there to decelerate such proclivity, that is, until mid-2018, when it proves to be already 'too little, too late'. What the IMF did not analyze, is what this author sees as the central theme: the increasingly impaired multiplier effect in the macroeconomic circular flow.

- **How the illusionist property sector is hollowing-out all other values**

China's behemoth SOEs continue to domineer over, rendering deleterious misallocation of resources for society as a whole. As they command all prerogatives in ways resembling a medieval robber-baron system, all the while they create comparatively meager contributions to the economy. China's SOE sector need to be visualized as the Party-Cadre sectors, or a system of corporate caste. From the standard Marshallian perspective in economics, one is able to visualize how much is the social deadweight necessitated by such system.

This institutional predisposition of China's is in no way to be dispelled, given the existent the country's unchallengeable Party-State system. Observing from what took place in longer than the past decade, it is highly evident that the omnipotent vested interest groups have all the powers it needs, to block any meaningful "reform" in ameliorating this most fundamental problems.

Here's the decisive structural difference in how the heavy indebtedness is incurred with the case of China, and with South Korea in the decades of the last century. With the property value of urban residents accounting for over 70% of China's average household asset (in large cities, this figure is nearly 80%), it demonstrates that, by incurring one of the biggest lumps in China's gargantuan debt piles, the hyper-development in the property market has crowded-out those industrial sectors that are more likely to advance the nation's overall industrial productivity and global competitiveness.

This is to be discerned in conjunction with the overwhelming large scale exoduses of foreign firms in the past 3 years, and one in six of China's own privately owned firms in the manufacturing sector went out of business in 2018 alone. These were mainly caused by the spiraling costs for the firms in recent years (which is much linked to the high property prices) plus the more recent US-China trade war - the arrival of a Judgment Day scenario, as it is a thing stemming from the fact that Beijing has never honored any of the promises made when China first joined the WTO for almost two decades.

China's is fundamentally different from what was in the case of South Korea decades ago when the country borrowed heavily for its industrialization. Fundamentally, the structural insidiousness intrinsic to China's economy was necessitated by the cumulative causation with a system where resource allocations are based on a least meritocratic measure.

The extremity in China's mirage property prices has, for longer than the last decade, enriched a new class of wealthy developers and related businesses that are less than 0.1% in the country's population, but hundreds of millions of the ordinary households, dubbed the "mortgage slave" households in China, are paying much more than half of their monthly disposable income to service their mortgage loans, having *most* (if not *all)* of their discretionary consumption stripped away from them. Through the post-2008 stimulus initiative and all the wherein derived expansionism funded by the state-owned banking system, those who have access to the prerogatives of funding (hence operate largely outside of the realm of economic activities that are subject to the discipline of the market) have amassed titanic amounts of wealth.

It is estimated by some of China's own economists that, these new super-rich, some one million households in the nation's population of 1.4 billion, now possess about half of all the liquid assets in the country, while a substantial majority in what can be categorized as the 'middle class' households steeps in the rut of having to expend more than half (in larger cities 60% and above is a usual portion) of their monthly income for their mortgage payments. Such is a recipe for an anemic middle class, and to those who have some basic knowledge in macroeconomics, one understands that such stratification negates future growth in household consumption and hence future growth in GDP.

Such anemic middle-class scenario - owing to such extremity in property valuations - was not the case in economic history when South Korea and Taiwan were playing the role of "The World's Factory" in the 1970s and 1980s, it was the emergence of a genuine middle-class stratum (in those decades, not suffering from the now China-type 'mortgage slave' symptom) in these societies that have underpinned the two countries' success story of economic transformation. And this is how one begins to see, what is dubbed as the "mortgage slave" phenomenon in China now casts a curse to the country's macroeconomic future. This book will show you why that is.

On average, the value of property accounts for 34.6% of the household assets in the US, this same figure for China is some whopping 70% and above, with urban residents. This figure of China's tells you a structural predicament in the nation's macroeconomic profile. This is because a majority of urban households' purchasing powers are being locked into the realm of transactions where revenues and expenses do not circulate toward industrial sectors that are more congenial to the advancement of the nation's overall productivity.

And this is one of the important causes to the country's sizable declines in corporate profitability in recent years. To be contrasted with, the US figure above tells you that a good-sized portion of the average household wealth is being channeled, through the workings of the equity markets and managed-fund markets, to sectors that are more congenial to the promoting of productivity growth economy-wide. The stories below will show you how China's equity markets have failed to function what is expected of its functionality - for the nation's economic prospect to be a benign one.

- **The untoward corporate profitability profiling is what makes China's debt problem perilous**

Entirely unreported by mainstream media in the west, is what an insider economist in China has revealed, telling the tale early this year that, among all profits realized by China's listed companies, two-thirds of it were gained by just the banks and the property developers. And, most companies in other sectors predominantly reported the entire amount of 'account receivables' as part of their profits. Such is a portrait for the kind of unhealthiest profiling on corporate profitability and how lawlessness accounting practices pervade in China.

In 2018, all of China's private-sector manufacturing firms, which consume relatively meager resources but provide many times of the employment than all the gargantuan, self-serving State-Owned Enterprises (SOEs), saw their average net profit slumped by 26%, and foreign firm in the same year reported an average decline of net profit by 9%. One in six of China's private-sector firms went out of business in 2018 alone, the year also saw an accelerated large-scale exodus of the foreign firms. These are the main factors that caused some 7.4 million unemployed workers returned to their rural homes in 2018.

While the average net profit for all manufacturing firms in China reported a 14% decrease, the robber-baron SOEs saw an average net profit increase of 8%. These decidedly portrait a deleterious undercurrent. That is, an overall picture of profitability lagging behind the rate of inflation by an enlarging gap. Such is *formulaic to a perilous denouement* - for the ubiquitous heavy indebtedness to become an increasingly broadening Ponzi-scheme phenomenon economy-wide: as the debtor entities are trapped in deficient earnings, they increasingly resorting to debt-rollover.

In the 2019 speech aforementioned, Xiang also points to the alarming facts that, in the total profit amount generated by all listed companies, " two-thirds of it were gained by just the banks and the property developers, and most other companies have all reported the entire amount of their 'account receivables' on the book as part of their 'profits'."

Worth repeating here from this speech, Xiang elaborates on what he dubbed *the "malignant" expansion toward indebtedness* in China, as a thing consequential to the institutionally-predisposed trait of corporate expansionism pervading the past decade: in that *"Corporations, in general, finance their expansions not predicated on their endogenous dynamism for growth, technological advancement, increase in profitability or retained earnings, but overwhelmingly relying solely on borrowings from the banking and shadow banking industries, as well as the issuance of corporate bonds that is now increasingly problematic".*

The prevailing mindset of *organized irresponsibility* with those who hold prerogative powers in China's nebulous institutional milieu is key to visualizing what's predominant in China's corporate realm: gaming the system for the actualization of 'gain privatized, and loss socialized'.

One more highlight for what's from aforesaid Xiang's speech, about "With that total profits made in 2017 by all listed companies, two-thirds of it were gained by just the banks and the property developers, and most of the other companies predominantly reported the entire amount of 'account receivables' as part of their 'profits'." As this author writes, this figure for 2018 was not yet out, but the difference would not be significant.

- **Institutional dyspraxia - it's not new, for China**

All these were caused by the intrinsically untoward institutional designs in China's semi-market economic system, wherein certain investment decisions are being made not subject to the discipline of the market. China's is an amorphous system where undue influences of all sorts come to negate the existence of accountability. Public resources are easily hijacked to serve the "gain privatized, and loss socialized" inequitable allotments in all shapes and forms. Such is necessitated by the institutional dyspraxia in China's pseudo-market economy, an inequitable milieu dominated by gargantuan, self-serving SOEs (including all major banks) commanding undue prerogatives rein in ways to distort what Economics 101 tells you about, the working of the price mechanism.

The best illustration for this is, in the past two decades, one of the main sources of revenue for China's colossal state-owned enterprises (SOEs) has been, profiting from re-lending the fund to privately-owned companies - that is, all the SOEs are entitled to huge amounts of low-interest loans from behemoth state-owned banks, and the

SOEs are free to lend these funds to privately-owned companies at a much jacked up rate of interest - it is ubiquitously the case that in general, privately-owned companies have so scarcely been approved by the state-owned banks (which comprise over 85% of China's banking industry capitalization). Such an economic system of China's is perhaps best dubbed as a *Bolshevik Mercantilist System*, the Party State's high-ranking bureaucrats are the new feudal lords and their terrain the SOEs the new fiefdoms.

Institutional dyspraxia, in which the SOE creates gigantic social deadweight is the manifestation of an ethos of institutionalized cronyism. And, this is certainly not new in China. To some extent China's Party-State system is analogical to the nation's dynastic system in antiquity. The last Ming Dynasty's effort to combat the marauding Manchu horsemen was the campaign of Sarhū (or, Sa-Er-Hu in the Chinese language) in 1619, where the 100-thousand-strong Ming army was (nearly) entirely slaughtered by the Manchu horsemen troops that was less than 30 thousands in number. The Ming Dynasty, a nation of over 80 million people with then (by far) the largest fertile arable land on earth, was overthrown by the united nomad tribes of Manchu, just a few million people in number.

History tells us, with Ming Dynasty's entrenched culture of corruptive bureaucrats and the institutionalized cronyism prevalent in its officialdom, these assured that the commanding field marshal appointed for that decisive battle was one of the most incompetent bureaucrat reigning.

- **How the property sector, substantially boosted GDP growth figures in past decades, is now turning into a curse to China's economic future**

To significant extents, China's GDP figures over the past two decades were boosted by the sectors (part of what Xiang (quoted earlier) called "blind expansionism") where substantial portions of investment or spending were *"not subject to the discipline of the market"*. Such non-market allocation of social resources boosted GDP figures in the year the spending/investment was made but carries very high opportunity costs in that, it entails too small a value in macroeconomic multiplier effect, and this necessarily negate future GDP growth.

Even as property developers have reaped huge profits in the past decade, the current average debt-to-equity (or net asset) ratio in the property sector is 80%, being the record high for the last 13 years. Vanke, one of the two most colossal property developers in China, has this ratio gone up to 84%, being the highest in its corporate history. How all these figures make sense in our macroeconomic scenarios?

If anything, the ongoing US-China trade war will only make such industrial ailments harder to ameliorate.

The extreme plethora of profligate property investments and inefficient capital expenditures that ended up with colossal, wasteful overcapacity. The importance in something being "wasteful" is to be understood by the centerpiece concept in economics, as the opportunity cost - wastefulness in capital expenditure necessarily entail too-small macroeconomic multiplier effect and that slashes future GDP growth.

China's "mortgage serfdom" economy today is one other big consequence stemming from aforesaid institutional dyspraxia

Since some years ago, the term "mortgage slaves" was coined and popularized amongst the common folks' online forums in China, depicting such pervasive phenomenon: with most homebuyers, more than half of the household income is spent just to meet the monthly mortgage payment (in certain first-tier cities, this figure can go as high as 70%).

Urban property prices, in general, have been pushed up to ranges that are so disproportionate to the average household income. This has been and still is, done with a permissive system for the **ubiquitous profiteering practices** of local governments in collusion with the developers. The biggest contributor to the surreal high prices is, without exception, one that is conspired by property developers and local government officials, whose political gains are hinged upon the GDP created of the year in his jurisdiction - both the sale of (the 70-year right to the use of) state lands and property developments create large increases in local GDP.

To give a quick example for said collusion, since some years ago the property developer who reaps the lion's share in property markets in the provincial capital of Hangzhou, the capital city of one of the two most economically advanced provinces in China, has been none other than the company owned by the mayor's wife. *Quasi-feudalistic constellations of this sort is the norm in China*, and they are not subject to Beijing's anti-corruption measures.

China, as a medium-income economy, with its GDP consisting about 15% of the World's GDP, has a total valuation in of its property markets amounting to about 25% of the world's total property values. If someone could manage to sell just all of the four most expensive cities' properties in China, at the current prices and exchange rate he/she can buy more than all of the properties in the entire United States. This shows the extent of surreal artificiality in China ultra-valuation.

To put things in a useful perspective, there are still over 200 million people in China (some 15% of the total population) live under what the World Bank has defined as the threshold income level for poverty - China's official figure shows this figure as 70 million as Beijing uses an utterly implausible threshold income level for this.

- **The currently popular saying in China, that the economy is being "abducted by the property market"**

As the "mortgage slave" households are now (commonly understood to be) in hundreds of millions strong, one more illustrative new term was coined in more recent years, giving a depiction that China's economy is now "abducted" by the surreal high prices in urban property markets.

The overall significance of this is:

As a vast majority of China's wage-earner households (in hundreds-of-millions) are being sucked dry in such hyper-inflated housing burden, policymakers in Beijing's high hope of transforming the economy towards one that's sustained by substantial increases in consumption as the economy's driving force now looks like a thing outright fictitious and unattainable.

Depicted in a video clip online with a popular You-Tube-style website in China: *"Innumerable families, who toiled their entire lives, ended up having all their fruition, their future, stripped away from them, reaped by those who hold vested interests in the property market - being transferred as obscene profits,* (This author: Chinese people call it the 'rampant profits' (Baoli)) *to those who command the distorted property market valuation. As most of people's on-paper 'wealth' in the property have in reality, been siphoned over, to the property moguls. This is the main cause of there being the lack of capability for (discretionary) consumption".* This author: the lacking of effective demand in a macroeconomic perspective is growth-negating for GDP.

In short, in China's existing system, being permissive to colluding property market manipulations, property pricing is nothing other than gouging. The consequence: household discretionary consumption is being stripped away from ordinary households, and what goes with it, the only hope for China to sustain a promising growth in future GDP.

Reality check: The purchasing of an urban property usually not only exhausts the fruition from an ordinary household's lifelong hard work, oftentimes it also claws in the lifetime savings from the household couple's parents (a cross-generation contribution to buying the disproportionately high-price condo just to afford the family's housing needs). Families having bought their dwellings is over-drafting decades of their future incomes.

Typically, ordinary people in China are steeped in heavy indebtedness (with their mortgage payments amount to more than half of their incomes, decades into the future) just to buy their own dwelling. Disproportionate high prices in the urban property have siphoned the financial blood in the main-street economy to an anemic state. It is increasingly evident in recent years that, this has caused the main-street economy to sunk into an irreversibly sluggish mode.

High prices in urban properties also hindered the young generation to reside in cities, rendering social mobility less probable. One other online commentary in China depicts: "The high property prices have rendered those who "were presumably the 'middle-class households' to become 'negative-equity class' in reality". Statistics in 2017 and 2018 show that dwindling discretionary consumption of the ordinary wage-earner households is growingly evident.

Such depiction is now a pervasive, much received understanding in China - regarding the ordinary people's current state of livelihood. If you read Chinese, you will easily come across myriads of commentators online here and there in China, holding generically similar views to the propositions mentioned above.

A number of academics and officials in Beijing have conceded to such dubbing of "abduction" and some openly made similar pronouncements with online video clips published in China's You-Tube-like web platforms, using the same, now-fashionable terms, saying that China's economy is now "abducted" by the property market.

Chapter 4

China's Debt Sinkhole, what's in store for global investor portfolios
The propagation of an "Illusionist" Economy

A main source of risk in equity investment in the world's major capital markets comes from a possible scenario of China's economy sinking into a vicious circle of shrinking GDP growth rate and structural unemployment, or worse, a state of stagflation. The majority of China's disproportionately colossal corporate and household debts are mainly incurred by non-viable property developments and gargantuan over-capacity in a number of industries. First, Heavy indebtedness in corporate China bears increasingly the recessionary weight on the economy. This, when combined with the probable further depreciation of China's currency (RMB) and other factors, is recipe for the economy to enter into a phase of stagflation, i.e. while economic growth continues to dwindle, the rate of inflation continues to rise.

Secondly, China's household debts are now nearing US$6 trillion, which is about half of the nation's 2018 GDP. For an economy where the GDP per capita is just about 16% t0 that of the United States, this incommensurate debt ratio is a pernicious macroeconomic condition.

The disproportionate debt loads with China's corporate entities and households are partly and almost totally, respectively, consequential to the "illusionist" economy created by China's asset-value hyperinflation, in urban property prices throughout the past decade.

While China's debt to GDP ratio is over 300%, the same figure for the US is just over 100%. And also importantly, in the US case the corporate debt portion is just about 70%, in contrast to China's figure, of nearing 160%.

Economists nowadays have generally failed to draw lessons from economic history for assigning plausible parameter values for their models. For instance, one important factor contributed to the Post-WWII economic boom in the US economy was that after the multiple years of en-mass military employment - where the government spends a lot and GIs don't have to pay for their living costs, hence hundreds of millions of people managed to accumulate sizable savings and then paid back their debts. The US's nationwide debt decreased from the pre-war period of about 100% to GDP, to just about half of the GDP. Other factors may be equally important, such how the US manufacturing sector has been so vastly strengthened and the Hirschman linkage effect it entails.

- **The new champion of growth - not in GDP, but in debts (Part 2)**

As China had since a few years ago no longer feature the GDP growth rate that leads the world, it has now assumed a new leading rate of growth: in corporate and household debts.

The day of reckoning has come, after the practicing in decades the debt-driven growth model as was depicted by Levin Zhu (quoted in previous chapters), where one trillion growth in GDP requires the increment of 6 trillion in debt.

The pace of debt increases now in China is double to that of the average rate of growth in debt world-wide. Since 2008 (what's dubbed as the starting year of the Great Recession), the rate of growth for increased indebtedness in China has been 12% on average, year after year.

The IMF highlighted China's impact on global financial markets in its October 2015 "Global Financial Stability Report": "The main spillover channels from China to the rest of the world remain economic growth and trade, but confidence channels and the direct financial linkages have also become stronger." This is now particularly more the case in the new era of the continuing US-China trade war scenario.

Repercussions between China's economic conditions and global financial markets are well outlined in aforesaid research: "*We believe that developed financial markets will, in all likelihood, overreact to deteriorating conditions in China. Part of the overreaction will be driven by expectations of further deterioration in emerging markets, especially if a continued slowdown in China corresponds to further depreciation of the RMB (China's currency). However, some of the overreaction will be driven by the inevitably greater focus of market participants on the latest headlines. As Nobel Laureate in Economics Daniel Kahneman has pointed out, the* availability of information that readily comes to mind affects how individuals formulate their investment views."

The Economist Panel at the Royal Swedish Academy of Sciences, which awards the Nobel Prize of Economics, had in 2002 awarded the Prize to Daniel Kahneman for his empirical findings challenging the assumption of human rationality prevailing in the more conventional approaches in economic theory. Kahneman's seminal contribution to behavioral economics, the Prospect Theory integrate cognitive science with economics, illustrating how the way people choose between probabilistic alternatives that involve risk. The theory states that people make decisions based on the potential value of losses and gains rather than the final outcome, and how heuristics, instead of the more conventional (some dubbed cookie-cutter-like) modular optimization that more conventional economic theorizing holds, is the effectual determinant.

The cognitive basis for common human errors arising from heuristics and biases established by Kahneman and Tversky is key to our understanding in how global financial markets are to react to the pending China factors in global investor portfolios. Notably in said IMF report on China: " limited transparency in the decision-making process and the rationale for certain policy measures heightens investor uncertainty, which inevitably reveals itself in the form of higher market volatility."

- **To what extent does China's economy matter, to the world?**

A research done by The Organization for Economic Co-operation and Development (OECD), entitled Outlook, estimates that a two percentage point decline in China's GDP may bring down the world's average GDP growth rate by 0.33% per year in the two-year time horizon. Said research also estimates, if such decline in the world GDP causes major financial markets in the world to undergo significant turmoil, two-percentage-point decrease in China's GDP growth may drag the world GDP growth down by 0.75% to 1% for the following two years.

The world economy's GDP growth rate in 2018 was 3.5%, so if China's GDP growth rate decreases by two percentage points, its impact to the world economy is estimated to be a fall in the global GDP growth rate in between 0.33% and 1%. That is, in the most pessimistic estimate of the impact is as large as a whopping 30.3% dive in the world economy's annual growth rate (from 3.5% to 2.5%) for the following two year. If we take a mid-point between the most optimistic (0.33%) and the most pessimistic (1%) estimates, which is 0.665%, then a two-percentage-point drop in China's growth rate will cause the world GDP to grow 19.5% slower.

In the above depiction, the low-end estimate of the China impact to the world (the world's growth down from 3.5% to 3.17%) can be simply ruled out, as this is a scenario where significant fall of China's GDP has no impact on major financial markets in the world. It is nowadays proven, for anyone to see that large drop in China's GDP will have substantial impact rattling the world's major financial markets.

Share prices are vulnerable to shocks in global economic conditions, the biggest firms are global: of the S&P 500 corporate sales in 2014, 48% were generated overseas. For the world's other major stock markets, big listed companies are also the most exposed to factors in global economic conditions.

- **Why does China's swelling corporate and household indebtedness matter so much, to future economic growth potentials?**

Some argues that South Korea in the 1980s and 1990s had also experienced disproportionate corporate indebtedness. This kind of argument fail to recognize a key difference in the Korean and the Chinese cases. The difference is made is akin to what's known in macroeconomics as Total Factor Productivity.

To wit, in the Korean case, the period of high corporate indebtedness came with continued rise in economy-wide productivity growth commensurate to the servicing of corporate debts - that is, the expenses in servicing of debts had continued to pay off, in the form of sufficiently high productivity gain economy-wide. In the case of China, the hikes in corporate indebtedness demonstrably elicit the opposite scenario.

Further, a majority of the indebted corporations in China are state-owned and they are entitled to prerogatives of a "robber-baron" kind: while they are taking huge de facto subsidies (with low-interest loans from state-owned banks), their poor profitability now does not even afford them to service the debts they've incurred in the recent past. Not only that, they actually do not need to service the debts, as all the state-owned banks will simply roll over these debts, lending to them the ever larger amounts of unpaid debts plus unpaid interests from previous years, year over year. This author characterizes such corporate scene of China's a 'corporate and financial caste system'.

Why is it that China's increased corporate indebtedness came alongside with a falling TFP? It is not hard to see: the absolute majority of all the gargantuan (nearing US$2 trillion) corporate debts incurred in the last 7 years or so went to investment projects in enormously oversupplied properties (you must have heard of the thousands of "ghost cities" in China), and colossal overcapacity in industries that necessarily entail China's dumping of various kinds products, the most important one being steel and hence conflicts in international trade with other major economies in the world, the US and the EU.

The dumping practice in international trade relating to steel is a particularly indicative case that illustrates China's mercantilist institutional outset. The White House has articulated as unfair trade practice, pointing to the fact that China's system of steel production has been free-riding on low standard labor safety and environmental considerations, to actualize the low prices that US and EU steel makers cannot compete. And, China's steel exports are able to feature such low prices with subsidies from the state, with a predatory agenda to cause steel makers in the US and EU to go out of business, aiming at the eventual monopolization of the global steel market.   China's state-owned steel maker are also subsidized by the low-interest loans lent by behemoth State-owned banks.

On the household indebtedness front, the first half of 2019 seen what hefty household indebtedness will feed-back in the macroeconomic circular flow, to slice corporate profitability. Reportedly, record-high inventories of consumers durables, hundreds of millions of unsold air conditioners, and substantially shrunken sales in fridges and TVs were being reported like never before in the last 2 decades. To billions of those households who considered themselves a member of the Middle Class, as their incomes now being drained by the mortgage payments that are much more than half of their monthly disposable incomes, they are now deprived of a majority of their discretionary consumptions. As was illustrated in previous chapter, this importantly lowers the macroeconomic multiplier effect and hence the economy's growth potentials.

- **GDP per capita matters**

Besides the key difference in said growth in economy-wide productivity dimension, the case of China also differ substantially from the South Korean case in that, the latter in the 80s and 90s already had per capita GDP that was multiple times higher than what's of China's today.

The more debts a country has accumulated, the more future incomes and corporate earnings must be expensed to pay for the principles and interests of the debt, which reduces both consumer and corporate expenditures. Macroeconomics 101 tells you, lower consumption and corporate expenditure necessitate lower rate of growth in GDP.

In America, debt is hurting young adults the most. Millennial say they are spending at least half their monthly paychecks on paying off debt (such as student loans). It was reported that, two years out of college, half of all graduates are still relying on their parents or other family members for some sort of financial help.

And, such indebtedness matters more in countries with lower GDP per capita than in countries with higher GDP per capita. indebtedness in youth does not drag down US economic recovery that much as, in comparison, the US GDP per capita is about 7 times higher than that of China's.

Now look at what will make China's economy so much dragged down by young and middle-age adults who spend typically from the low end of 50% to the high end of about 70% (for those live in the first-tier cities such as Beijing, Shanghai, and Shenzhen) of their income on mortgage payments.

As the prospect of China's economy now calls for significant increases in consumer spending, the phenomenal high proportion of income sunk month after month into mortgage payments as articulated above demonstrates a stark reality of the roadblock. The enlarging-middle-class scenario touted by Beijing in painting rosy picture for China's progression in making consumption the new engine for economic growth now increasingly ring hollow.

A 2017 Goldman Sachs report points out: "China is more likely to follow Japan's path than South Korea's: debt will continue to grow to higher levels ... just like Japan, we believe China will eventually face a period of much slower growth, especially if it delays moving ahead on the structural reforms ... The problem for China is that Japan entered its period of slow growth as a much richer country in 1990, with a GDP per capita that was 2.5 times as high as that of China today."

This book will show you how a majority of such "structural reforms" is not forthcoming, or becoming too late, too little a thing to avert the probable scenario for the economy to enter into a stagflation phase.

People in the global money-managing and accounting spheres with major-league entities like Goldman Sachs and Ernest Young will not tell you some of the most important truth. Why? They have their vested interests in not revealing some of the most alarming facts, for fear of losing their market shares in providing their financial services to Beijing.

- **The Incremental Capital-Output Ratio - "a headwind three times as strong as it was ten years ago"**

In a January 2019 article published by The Brookings Institute, Joyless growth in China, India, and the United States, Indermit Gill, Senior Fellow at Global Economy and Development states: "... perhaps a big reason for the joylessness of growth is the increasing difficulty of converting saving into output. Since 2007, the incremental capital-output ratio (ICOR) in China has tripled from 3 to 9, while the growth rate of GDP has fallen by half. The Chinese people are still saving a bunch, but investment is paying off less and less. Imagine trekking into a headwind three times as strong as it was ten years ago; it would make a pleasant hike into a painful slog." This is not the only article that you may come across, showing you that predicaments in Chinas' future path is evidenced by continued deterioration in ICOR.

In 2008, China's money supply (measured as M2) was 47.5 Trillion RMB, ten year later, this figure has come to 170 Trillion, which is larger than the US and EU's money supplied of the year combined. This illustrates the failure in managing indebtedness by lifting economy-wide productivity and hence corporate debtors is capable of repay their debts through increased profitability and households through their increased incomes. With the gargantuan, self-serving, grossly inefficient robber-baron SOE sector monopolizing some two-thirds of the nation's resources, productivity gain from private sector firms cannot but be too limited to lift the boat.

Hence what Beijing did has been managing the high-speed debt railing swoosh by the ever-enlarging money supply of M2. The gargantuan indebtedness is then transferred through colossal increments of M2, to ordinary households in the form of hyperinflation in property prices, and substantial price hikes in a majority of necessity consumer goods, such as food and medicines.

Nihon Keizai Shimbun, the Japanese equivalent of Wall Street Journal (where we get our Nikkei index for the Japanese stock market), reported in August 2019 that China's household indebtedness has exceeded US$ 6.5 Trillion, such is an enormously outsized proportion given China's current GDP-per-capita level. And how this hefty indebted deprive ordinary households' discretionary consumption is demonstrated by *China's historically highest inventory level seen in 2019, with all consumer durables such as air conditioners, fridges, TVs etc,* as a vast majority of ordinary household consumers are being sucked dry just to pay for their mortgage with the hyper-inflated condo prices. Increasing unemployment expectable of the many structural problems in the economy will only heighten such trend. Ordinary households are now increasingly feeling the pinch from burdens in repaying the mortgage and car loans.

And, as a host of consumer electronics firms in China have been substantially subsidized by the government, colossal drops in sales will exacerbate existing problems of lacking in competitiveness.

The metaphor quoted earlier " a headwind three times as strong as it was ten years ago" also so pertinently depicts what ordinary households in China are now facing.

In 1999, China's then Prime Minister Zhu Ronji established 4 asset management corporations to take over the 1.4 Trillion RMB long-standing bad loans from the 4 state-owned banks. It was mainly with the so-called Debt-to-Bond swap, in other words, having had everyone in China, from new-born bay onward, sharing about 1000 RMB to swallow it. Or, as many said, China has managed to have "grown out" of that bad debt problem that time.

That 1.4 Trillion RMB bad loan was about 16.7% of China's 1999 GDP. With the national debt that's over 300% of the 2018 GDP currently (and keep increasing), China's existing bad loans could easily go nearing or over 100% of the 2018 GDP when the 'day of reckoning' scenario, relating to China's US$20-Trillion-sized shadow banking industry, comes: *""No one knows who owes what to whom or how much, only when it starts to go bankrupt will things start falling apart."* as depicted by economics professor at the University of Toronto, Peter Pauly. It will be a China sinkhole that rattles the world.

You don't need in-depth knowledge in economics to see that this time, China is not going to be possibly growing out of its debt problems, like what was in 1999.

Chapter 5

An economy sustained by a modality of 'Abracadabra Valuation'

How 'mortgage serfdom' is pawning China's economy to a pernicious future

China is the world's number one again, besides having been the nation with the largest population since antiquity. Unfortunately, the number one we now articulate here is surely not good news for the country's economic future.

China, with a GDP *per capita* that's about 16% to that of the United States', now ranks the world's number one in a set of housing unaffordability indexes. China's property price to median-income ratio now way exceeds all of the high-income economies in the developed world. And this renders the country with *some rather inescapable macroeconomic consequences.*

Three of China's largest cities now feature the world's highest housing unaffordability indexes. The ratios: counted by the median price for an average-size urban condo to the annual median household dispensable income in Beijing, Shanghai, and Shenzhen are 66.36 times, 62.8 times, and 57.34 times respectively. In most of China's larger cities, condo prices have been inflated to extremely unaffordable levels to median-income households.

These ratios are very much *the highest among all major economies* in the world. And, the macroeconomic implication in this, is, in reality, one of the most potent elements determining the nation's economic future.

- **A property price collapse is preventable, at high costs**

Such ratios, of around 60%, signifies the ultra-high housing burden a vast majority of China's middle-class households face. This chapter will show how this will make a real, parametric difference in terms of its macroeconomic consequences. Widely observed in China's economy throughout 2018, and continued into 2019, is the sizable downgrading in middle-class household consumption.

With such ultra-high ratios above, how would the banks in China (with the absolute majority of them state-owned) be so comfortably making mortgage loans to all those property purchases? The reason being: the banks are betting on the average property prices and the borrowers' incomes to keep going up, such that the mortgage borrowers' 'equity' value is deemed to commensurate to an artificially "benign" prospect.

One figure that enables you to see how such 'property price hyperinflation' of China's came about is, for longer than the last two decades China's M2 (broadly defined money supply) has been growing at an average rate of 20% per annum, which is much more than twice that of the average annual GDP growth rate.

The macroeconomic profiling of the M2 growth rate above will, anywhere else in the world, necessarily mean high inflation in the economy, how is it that we haven't seen that happening in China, till early 2019?

Zhou Xiao chuan, the former chairman of China's central bank (PBOC) conceded prior to his retirement in 2018, that the gargantuan excesses in money supply have been much 'absorbed' by the gargantuan property price bubbles being the secret recipe in keeping the consumer price inflation in check.

Not revealed by Zhou was the one other factor: as mentioned in Chapter 1, China's CPI index is perhaps the only one in the world that *excludes* residential property prices as an element in the calculation. It is arguably sensible if one argues that Beijing's National Stats Bureau's treating residential housing as an item of "investment" and not "consumption" being *deleteriously manipulative a thing* in nature.

However, the property bubble that has prevented all the excessive M2 to become inflationary in consumer prices, is likely to be a Faustian Bargain in the end.

Beijing is now in a tie-in bundle, in that it has to sustain such a bubble state - a collapse in property prices will render collaterals in the hundreds of millions of mortgage contracts to flip into a state of negative equity, therein causing financial implosions economy-wide.

The reader will see from later chapters what's in store for the nation's economic future with such modulation, of running the economy with, what this author dubs, a pawn-shop logic.

In case of a severe property market downturn, how the banks see it is, if the condo prices go down by more than 35% of the initial price when the loan was made (which is the prevalent down-payment provision for condo buying in China) and the borrower fails to make the mortgage payment, the banks can simply sell the condo.

This means, similar to what was in the US banking industry prior to the 2007 start of the subprime crisis, China's banks *do not* much take into account what dire systemic risk there is when all the banks in the country are conducting such untoward module of operation - even as all the major-league banks are state-owned.

This book will show how likely the following scenario is to pan out: a *reflexive* feedback loop necessitated by the current ailments in the corporate realm (characterized by hefty corporate indebtedness and shriveling corporate profitability) and untoward prospects in the consumer realm (of the downgrading of consumption that permeates the middle class) is there to substantially jack up the rate of unemployment and further suppress incomes.

Reportedly, from 2018 and continued into 2019, we have already witnessed a pervasive downgrading in consumption across the board, with what can be considered the middle-class households in China.

China's economy is now sustained by an 'Abracadabra valuation' modality in its property markets.

Beijing has in the last two years realized the imminent colossal danger in such systemic risk and started to implement curbs to price hikes in property markets, meanwhile also dish out measures in preventing the property prices from collapsing. Such collapse-prevention measures being of the highest priority as, the emergence of collapse means the entire banking system will bust - as the banks' collateral values with their mortgage loans will tank, with household borrowers in hefty negative equity.

So actually, with China's Party-Sate economic system, Beijing may for some time have the command to all institutional leverages it needs to prevent the property prices from collapsing. However, the gigantic (what you've learned from economics 101 tells you about the) opportunity cost to be paid for this is devilish in the median-to-long-run: as it *severely debilitates the consumption component in the GDP equation*, then through the working of the macroeconomic circular flow, corporate profits are more likely to continue with its current declining trend started longer than 2 years ago and the rate of unemployment keeps increasing.

In short, with China's Party-State system, preventing the property market from collapsing is achievable, at the price of pawning the nation's economic future to a pernicious designation, and a probable denouement of stagflation, with Beijing's immediate and continuing needs in disallowing the market mechanism to correct itself of such asset-price inflation.

● **Disenfranchisement of the middle-class, and its macroeconomic consequences**

Beijing may be able to prevent the property market from collapsing, but the inescapable bigger problem necessitated is the disenfranchisement of the middle class.

Then the real issue is actually **not** whether if there will be a collapse of the property market in China, but what *dire consequences* there are, with Beijing's being *capable of preventing* the property market from collapsing.

Let's now put the non-owner households in the picture: For renters in those aforesaid cities, the equivalent figures for the burdens in renting a home are not too dissimilar to those who are sustaining a mortgage payment. In February 2019, the average rent-to-income ratio in the three cities of Beijing, Shenzhen, and Shanghai are 63%, 59.3%, and 49.8%. So there is virtually no escape, in all bigger cities, such figures simply mean: a swath of what can be seen as the Middle Class in China have that big a chunk of their incomes for consumption gobbled away by the burdens of housing.

Hence, such extreme housing unaffordability has, in effect, the equivalent of *a steep poll tax* on housing. And, the *macroeconomic consequence from this is in actuality much worse than having an actual poll tax on housing*. This is because, if the incomes ripped from consumer households were done by imposing a poll tax to equivalent amounts, the money will go to the government as huge revenues, and that could enable the public sector to implement things like supply-side policies that are beneficial to the economy's growth potentials.

In US history, Poll taxes enacted in Southern states between 1889 and 1910 had the effect of disenfranchising a majority of African American as well as poor whites, as payment of the tax was a prerequisite for voting right. Hyperinflation in China's property prices is *much worse* than levying the equivalent amounts of poll tax:

First, it not only *disenfranchise* a swath of middle class households by ways of taking away a range of discretionary consumption they otherwise are capable of having - thus cuts off a huge chunk of the consumption element in our GDP equation, which is requisite to a *benign macroeconomic multiplier effect* and therein the economy's growth potential.

To interpret the above jargon in macroeconomics: as the hundreds of millions of home-buyer households are all paying much more than half of their monthly disposable income to service their mortgage loans, it is having *most* (if not *all)* of their discretionary consumption stripped away from them. This substantially lowers what is called in macroeconomics the *Marginal Propensity to Consume (MPC)* and hence make the all-important *multiplier effect* to get substantially short-changed.

Secondly, at the same time, not only that it does not enhance government revenue (like what the levying of an actual poll tax will), the middle-class households impoverished by the burdens of housing means fewer tax revenues from sales taxes.

Thirdly, the ultra-thin layer of households enriched by the ultra-profits in property-related businesses, together with the now much more stratified economic demography, has an inescapable macroeconomic consequence, of the shrinking *MPC* and hence the short-changing of the all-important multiplier effect - a key determinant in the economy's growth potential.

Given the already overextended investment spending as a component in the nation's GDP equation for the last decade, and the prospect of trade-war related factors that negate future net-exports, the consumption component in our macroeconomics GDP equation, is now exactly what China's last hope lies, in sustaining future growth potentials.

As this author will illustrate, such ultra-high housing burdens is a thing consequential to the state of (what this author dubs) institutional dyspraxia with the country's hodgepodge semi-market economic system. In a genuine market economy, no such abracadabra-valuation mode can be sustained to such an extent.

So how do young couple households with a median-income get the 35% down-payment fund to get approved for their mortgage loans in these cities? Here's the story of, what's being dubbed in China, the *"Six-Purse"* phenomenon.

- **The Six-Purse overdraft for housing - the China version of 'subprime' mortgages**

How does anyone with an income not dissimilar to the median income, depicted at the start of this chapter, in China's larger cities qualify for a mortgage?

It is done with the so-called *Six-Purse endeavor* - a cross-generation all-out overdraft practice that is now pervasive among the younger generation home-buyers. That is, in the household, the couple and their parents (on both sides) will all need to empty their bank accounts (the "purse") to contribute toward the down-payment - typically 35% of the condo's purchase price.

In the 2005-2007 American subprime mortgage loan scenarios, the most dramatic case at the time was dubbed a "NINJA" mortgage loan - the banks were approving mortgages for people who are in a financial state of *"No Income, No Job, No Asset"*, as everyone is betting on the continuation of the property bubble to go on forever - and the banks felt very comfortable with the financial derivatives that enabled them to have, on surface, moved all the financial risks incurred from all subprime deals *off their balance sheet*.

The China case, of the Six-Purse contrivance illustrated above, has in it an element that's analogical to the so-dubbed NINJA mortgage. Instead of the banks being comfortable about moving risks off their balance sheets via the fraudulent designs in those financial derivatives to achieve organized irresponsibility - central in the American case - in the China case, it is the institutional configurations in the country's financial industry that are permissive of organized irresponsibility. The propagation of this China-version of 'subprime' mortgage is with an entirely different untoward mechanism.

In both cases, surreal financial transactions were being facilitated in omnipresent fashion and they necessarily coagulate-cascade economy-wide, toward systemic risks. Nevertheless, the China case may prove to be far more disruptive a 'euthanasia' to the nation's economic growth potential in the end - given that, for political reasons (of maintaining the perceived legitimacy of the Party-State system), Beijing will, and has all the institutional leverage it needs (at least for the short-to-median-run time horizon), to prevent a property market collapse, from its current abracadabra height.

The banks are not worried about the fact that a median-income household borrower managed to garner that 35% down payment not from their own earning powers, but through aforesaid all-out overdraft practice that *depletes* all said six savings accounts in two generations. Owing to the decades of "single-child" policy, typically young people in China who have come of age in purchasing their own dwellings get unconditioned supports from their parents - such is considered a norm in the mainland-China culture. And, without any sibling in the family, there is no competition in such cross-generation drawing of resources.

Such China-version of the Subprime Mortgage is now preeminent in the country. What it necessitates is this: as a swath of middle-income households are on high leverages (typically expending 50% or more of both of the couple's disposable incomes to meet their monthly mortgage payment, for their urban dwellings. Plus, with those who make much less than the median income and could not come up with that 35% down payment for reasons such as their parents are in the rural regions (hence are having comparatively paltry income and savings).

As employment situations become increasingly less benign, thanks to a *reflexive* death-spiral of high corporate indebtedness, shriveling profitability, and the foreign manufacturing firms' (importantly including those that are from Taiwan) titanic-scale exodus, the heightened systemic risk in China's financial markets has entered uncharted waters like never before..

And therein, with the debt loads that's now to the tune of 300% of GDP (and it's over 300%, if we use what Beijing's high finance sphere insider, Levin Zhu, has revealed, reported in Chapter 2) with an economy that features a GDP *per capita* that's about 16% to that of the US, such picturing portrays for the increasing fragility of the nation's economy.

To be noticed here, Japan has an economy that also features a very high Debt-to-GDP ratio. But, the important qualitative difference here is that Japan's is without the threat of an ultra-valuation property market, Japan's property market collapse in 1990 was allowing the market mechanism to correct itself. And its GDP per capita being way above what's of China's, plus the one important fact that people the world over fail to see, that is, the very substantial earnings repatriation from corporate revenues overseas - hence even as the economy is now still, in part, mired in a deflationary state, the kind of structural fragility illustrated above, with the China case, is not present.

To most people's surprise, if we use the GNP (Gross National Products) instead GDP (Gross Domestic Products) as measurement for the nation's economy, Japan's GNP (that is, GDP plus the nation's overseas revenues from corporate and individual investments) today is not that much smaller than that of China's.

It is true, that property price hikes and the home-buying push it generates (an entrenched expectation that the property prices can only go ever higher, expedited the transactions) have also helped to boost property- sector-related consumption all along the way in China, for at least the past decade. However, for reasons this book will demonstrate to you, such consumption-engendering effects have now proved to be so much eclipsed by the consumption-deterring effects - as the ultra-valuation in China's property market takes away typically *much* more than half of the household's disposable income. In China's three largest cities, a majority of middle-class households who bought their condos within the last decade are paying typically around 65-75% of their disposable incomes monthly for their mortgage, in all larger cities (where most of the jobs are located) said figure (the ratio of mortgage payment to household income) easily exceeds 50%.

- **What could come out of Beijing's dirigisme**

One is to be reminded, of what made the US subprime bubble to burst - a precipitous downturn in price will quickly put the subprime borrower household in a state of *negative equity*. When China's mortgage debtor households face unemployment, there is nothing to sustain the mortgage payment - with China's spurious 'social insurance' scheme's unemployment benefit that pays for less than 10% of an average household's realistic living costs, and the couple's parents' savings were already depleted for the 35% down payment at the start.

However, with China's Be-all and End-all system of dirigisme, which defines the Party-State's pseudo-market economic system, this property price bubble is crucial, in the maintaining of what this author dubs *the Pawn-Shop economy*, the Party-State is to leverage everything to prevent the most gigantic property bubble in history from bursting. And, that is exactly where the bigger problem lies - that the bubble will be sustained at all costs, by the operations of the statecraft.

That is, *without the bursting* of the property bubble, the property prices stay at their abracadabra heights is to increasingly undermine the nation's macroeconomic viability. As Beijing's authoritarian system commands all institutional leverages, quite possibly it is capable of preventing the burst, at the price of bigger macroeconomic ailments, among which, the worst scenario of stagflation may be in the card.

This is because, while hefty mortgage burdens continue to retard much of the middle-class households' discretionary consumption. To avoid the onset of a deflationary trend, China's central bank had in 2018 started to implement policies that enable the corporate world to re-leverage, gearing up the money supply, measured by M2.

A ratcheting mechanism of feedback is now set, and the ultra-high property prices are to continue, it allows the ratcheting up by no less than the rate of inflation. The China-version of the subprime property market has *a denouement that is very different from the American version of subprime.* A more probable future scenario is to be a protracted macroeconomic path of dwindling growth and increasing unemployment. As was mentioned in the last chapter, a consensus among many of China's own economic researches indicates that for every one percentage point drop in China's GDP growth rate, there will be the loss of around 8 million jobs in the economy.

This book will demonstrate what eventuating macroeconomic scenario there is in the card. Our macroeconomic linchpin issue here is, to visualize how the *multiplier effect* is to be the factor of parametric primacy.

Chapter 6

An economy where "The tail is wagging the dog"

The hyperinflation in property prices is a poll tax in disguise

To what extent China's "mortgage serfdom" will deprive the nation's economy of a benign future? We need to get a panoramic view of China's unique Party-State economic system and make sense from such systemic purview.

For the entire past decade, Beijing's fiscal and monetary policies were much addicted to mere expediency measures at the cost of probable detriments such measures necessarily entail, to long-run economic growth. Consequentially, having so over-drafted with virtually all ammunition that can be made available in future for macroeconomic management, it looks highly probable that China's policymakers are facing some sharply diminishing effectiveness with fiscal and monetary means they could muster. To prevent the collapse in property prices, Beijing's policy prioritizing now looks increasingly more like a system where "The tail is wagging the dog".

The first underpinning rationale in how China's future economic growth potential is to be gauged is straight forward - to those who have some basic knowledge in macroeconomics. *(For readers who are not equipped with this knowledge, an appendix at the end of this book provides a quick illustration that may be used to fill this knowledge gap)*

A secular trend in China's path of development was, arguably, set in the post-2008 period, and its underlying momentum was expedited in more recent years. The key issue in this is the continued intensifying of income inequality and fast-growing household debts - in which the stratum of Middle-Class households see their disposable income dwindling owing to the continued ratcheting up in urban property prices and rents. These are manifestations of the most extreme form of financialization of the economy in China, capitals are being moved out of manufacturing industries in titanic scales, into property market speculation.

This ultra-valuation in urban property markets, by substantially eating away much of middle-class households' disposable income, necessitates a *parametric shift* that severely negates a benign scenario for the economy's growth potential. This is through the working of a fundamental mechanism in our macroeconomic model, the multiplier effect. That is, a   middle-class household stratum in the economy with a substantial chunk of their incomes eaten away by the extraordinary high housing cost necessitates a degraded multiplier effect as decreasing disposable income necessarily lead to a shrinking *Marginal Propensity to Consume (MPC)*.

- **A parametric shift**

The aforesaid parametric shift in the country's macroeconomic configuration is of utmost centrality in gauging China's economic future. And, such thematic focus is seriously under-researched or neglected by most economic researches on China today.

As was briefly mentioned in Chapter one, for the 3 years to the end of 2018, China's *household indebtedness has increased by* about *22.2% of the nation's 2018 GDP* (which is circa 20 Trillion RMB) while the *consumption element in the GDP equation has decreased* by some 3.3% of the country's 2018 GDP - percentage-wise it may not seem big, but the importance in this, is that it signifies the *reversal of a secular trend* China's economy has had for two decades - of a steady growth of the consumption component in the GDP equation, that is much needed especially for the current stage of the economy, where all other previously overstretched engines of growth now turn increasingly ineffective, fast. This reversal signals for the start of a *downturn in the consumption component of GDP like never before*.

This is the *manifestation of a deteriorating MPC scenario*. And, such downgrading in consumption is now of particular weight in determining China's economic growth, as other components in the GDP equation, capital investments and government spending, have demonstrably all come near their points of saturation hence increasingly ineffective - while the one other GDP component, net-exports of China's, is now heading for a rough ride in the backdrop of the on-going US-China Trade War.

A rather famed (US-trained) economist in China, Dr. Feng Xiaonian in a 2018 speech pointed to how conventional fiscal and monetary policy measures have both seen fast diminishing effectiveness in their implementations (in how they have intended to boost the consumption components in the GDP), it is a phenomenon widely observed and reported in China. What Feng and other Think-Tank grade economists in China have failed to identify as the main cause in this is the dwindling MPC and therein the shrinking multiplier effect.

This, the size of the MPC and the so derived multiplier effect is pivotal, and it is a much unduly ignored determinant in most researches on China's economy.

This author points out, the MPC/multiplier effect theme is the canonical parametric determinant formulated by the founder mathematician of our macroeconomic model. Albeit that economists around the world make all their inferences in macroeconomic research basing on this model, the macroeconomic causations relating to variations in the MPC is a much under-researched field. One reason for that being, it is a much institutionally-determined parameter, and mainstream academic economists in the last 3 decades have mostly shied away from incorporating institutional issues in their research and simply take it as an exogenous variable. The institutional learning in academic economics for longer than the past 3 decades was virtually extinct, not being taught in perhaps 99% of all the Ph.D. programs in North America for decades.

For some half a century, mainstream economists around the world have by and large shied away from institutional issues relevant to our macroeconomic modeling. To this author, decreasing MPC is the most pivotal parameter in macroeconomic research on China. Yet, research undertakings by the global investment banking/brokerage industry and the academia alike have generally failed to give insight into this issue of centrality. So are researches conducted by China's own think tanks.

The second underpinning rationale in gauging China's economy is an argument known in certain fields in science as "sub-optimal solutions may lead to bigger problems". Beijing is now *walking the tight rope of a 'Tri-lemma"* - there is the impossibility of a monetary and fiscal policy mix capable of serving the three conflicting macroeconomic objectives of: salvaging the dwindling consumption component in the GDP equation, preventing the emergence of 'negative equity' with the hundreds of millions of home-buyer households and hence a China-version of 'subprime' crisis, and sustaining employment. Meanwhile, this book will show what Beijing has claimed as the "supply-side policy" being inherently fallacious and void.

And, out of said three objectives, the second one poses the biggest and most imminent threat and hence will be given priority over the others. In this arena, Beijing is compelled to take various sub-optimal solutions. And, these will not only be insufficient in solving the problems but also create new problems.

With China's property market and mounting household and corporate debts, Beijing is now in a position of being unable to go for an optimal solution, which is, like what the US government did in the subprime crisis. And, the patches of Beijing's sub-optimal solutions now implementing is capable of eventuating in colossal predicaments to China's needed economic growth.

- **The interplay of middle-class consumption downgrading and shriveling corporate profitability**

As a majority of home-buyer households in China now have to typically spend *much more than half* of their incomes just to meet their mortgage payments, it cuts off a sizeable portion in the discretionary consumption they otherwise may have had - that's how the term "mortgage slaves" became popular in China in recent years.

With a majority of China's urban households being "mortgage slaves", as is evidenced by recent statistics earlier, it necessitates the downgrading of middle-class consumption, and this then in turn necessarily loops back in the circular flow to aggravate shriveling corporate profitability.

That is, as the high property prices are extremely disproportionate to average incomes, burdens with housing - with urban renters   of homes in China's larger cities also paying disproportionate portion (between one-third to half) of their incomes for housing - is rendering (what's termed in macroeconomics) the effective demand to dwindle, it then inescapably a curse for shriveling corporate profitability economy-wide.

Such demographic profiling for said state of debilitation, in what can be seen as China's middle-class stratum importantly mean, that the *multiplier effect* in our universally valid macroeconomic model will be much short-changed to extends that are likely to be too small to sustain meaningful GDP growth, in being capable of offsetting the impacts from the US-China trade war - wherein the perceived tariffs hikes, together with the fast-increasing costs of manufacturing in China having already caused an array of major-league foreign firms exited China, bringing with them an entire supply chain of manufacturers.

This deficient multiplier effect is also to be seen in a diachronic perspective: in recent years (and still the case today) about one-third of China's GDP is attributable to transactions in the property market, with all the ghost cities and unsold properties, a big chunk of the GDP creation in the last decade have been cut off in their (extended-round) flow-on in the macroeconomic circular flow, and hence the corresponding multiplier effect. For readers not having the basic knowledge in macroeconomics, an explanation to this issue in this book's appendix may be of some help.

Given that China's property transactions now worth one-third of the nation's GDP (such is a thing unprecedented in the entire economic history of the humankind), this peculiarity is to be perceived in the context of the nation's debts now amounting to about 260% (or much over 300%, if you think Levin Zhu, the aforementioned insider in China's sphere of high finance has got a better gauge) of its 2018 GDP.

Some estimates indicate that if debts with the shadow banking industry are included, China's debt figure exceeds 400% of its 2018 GDP). In short, the extreme overvaluations in the property sector with the consequential, hundreds of millions of "mortgage slaves", now significantly jeopardizes the economy's future GDP growth potentials.

A majority of economists the world over (such as those at the IMF) have failed to be keenly aware of the one fundamental fact that, with China's Party-state mercantilist economic system (where significant portions of the economy is *"not subject to the discipline of the market"*), the year-on-year figures in China's GDP are by nature not much meaningful when comparisons are made with the year-on-year GDP figures in genuine market economies of the west - at least in terms of the rate of growth. A sizeable sector that is *"not subject to the discipline of the market"*, such as what's in the China case, is capable of forging current GDP figures at the cost of long-run objectives - the economy's future growth potential. This is in actuality the all-important implication China's hefty corporate and local government indebtedness has, to the nation's economic future.

The root cause for China's economic predicaments now rests in the fact that the system is in a Hodgepodge semi-market setting.

First, a significant portion of the economy is run by behemoth state-owned, over-privileged corporations, whose decision making in investments are (ultimately)*"not subject to the discipline of the market"*.

Secondly, for two decades or so local government finances have so heavily relied on the monetization of state land and there is the ubiquitous collusion between local bureaucrats and property developers, to facilitate price hikes in the property market. These have been posing forces of distortion in incentive alignments economy-wide.

- **"The high prices of property is just a poll tax in disguise"**

An online financial talk show commentator in China that lately gained much popularity branded herself as Weicheng, uttered some strikingly cogent comments regarding the current state of China's property market: "From the very start, the commoditization of housing was born with the gene of immorality." This author: China's *was* a self-claimed "socialist system", wherein housing properties *were* owned by the state. There was the Property 'Reform' started some 2 decades ago launched in China's property market, since then it is stipulated that *the right of use* (not the actual ownership) in properties are owned by individuals for 70 years.

What is this "gene of immorality" about? The comment goes on: "It is the taxing on people's birthright, entitled to a place of abode. In history, people have loathed things like a poll tax, *the high prices of property are just a poll tax in disguise.*"

This author offers the following allegory:

In America's Post-Civil War era, the poll tax emerged as one of the techniques used by southern whites to disenfranchise African Americans for their voting rights. In the increasingly stratified society in China (with the GINI index is one of the highest in the world), the kind of ultra-valuation with urban properties is, in effect, equivalent to a poll tax to "disenfranchises" an enormous layer in society, households who pay much more than half of their disposable incomes just to service the mortgage for their residential condos, away from being a member of the Middle Class stratum in society - with the most plausible definition for the term Middle Class household: a household who is capable of making discretionary (or, much more than just subsistence) consumption.

This author points out, one of the fundamental tenets from the onset of the Communist rule in China, in 1949, has been a self-claimed system of socialism that eliminates private property - any substantial asset are to be owned only by the state. 1979 saw the start of the Economic Reform, it is now amply evident that the property markets in China have been the most egregious, titanic poaching operations that have demolished the last trace of social equitableness. It is engineered in the name of "reform", by vested interest groups who hold undue prerogatives. It has created a state of "mortgage serfdom" for hundreds of millions of households in the country.

Said online commentator went on: "High prices in property markets is a tumor, if you peer off its outer layers, you will discover that the very core in it being the "Land auctioning system".

This author: as all lands in China are owned by the state, it was since some two decades ago that the auctioning and selling of the right (of 70 years) to use urban land for property construction has become the mainstay for local government finance around the country. And, the evolution of this system has gone on a path permissive of utter malfeasance, worthy of the depiction from said commentator - "a societal tumor".

Thus our lady commentator concludes: "To get the highest bidder, the state had created a type of market exactly where such type of market should not be in existence, where people lost their prior housing rights and a class of property moguls reaping colossal wealth was bred. One after another story of crime engraved in the land".

This author restates the gist in this: a property market where prices are unduly calibrated by such veritable heist of *the highest bidder mechanism*, in the absence of enforcement of the competition law (China did enact one such law, and no different from what was with most of all the other laws in China, it was never being enforced for the purpose proposed in such legislation), it has become an arena full of abuses and profiteering. China did copy its Competition Law from Taiwan, the problem is, it's never been enforced for what the law is designed for. The only case where the law was being enforced were actually motivated by the relevant authority's abusive intent, which was trying to use this law for some false claims against certain large foreign firms' operations in China, while any real monopolistic conduct of China's lumpy state corporations has always been immune to this law.

Said nefarious, fake Anti-monopoly clampdowns against foreign firms in China were in clear violation of the WTO rules, yet before the Trump administration's actions from 2018, none of any western investor nations in China had ever done anything effectual as a response. Apart from the United States, to any developed nations in the world, China was simply "too big to question".

- **An Ultra-Valuation Trap**

To highlight the causation chain in how China's property market comes to what it is today: The state-ownership of land has enabled local governments to finance all their colossal public work buildups, and among all these, quite sure a lot more than half of them are "white elephant" public works - and hence will not serve any (what's known in macroeconomics as the) supply-side fiscal policy purposes in helping to lift median-term productivity of the economy.

That is, among all the overdraft financing of the local governments that have created a big chunk of China's GDP throughout the past two decades, a lot more than half of them have virtually a zero rate of return, to the economy as a whole. And, taking into consideration what's central to the *canonical rationales in economics*, the *opportunity costs* and the *crowding-out effect*, this rate of return is in actuality very much a negative one. This book will show, how the module of monetizing the state-ownership of land - where the chain of abracadabra valuation in China's property markets start - has now turned into a curse, to the nation's economic future.

Here is what this author called the Ultra-valuation Trap:

Tian Guoli, Chairman to China Construction Bank (one of the five state-owned, major-league banks in China) in a January 2019 public speech pointed to the fact that the total valuation of all properties in China now stands at about US$40 Trillion, while current valuation for all US properties is at about just US$30 Trillion (which is about 150% of the 2018 US GDP). This figure of US$40 Trillion given by Tian is very much an underestimate from the currently widely recognized and quoted figure of RMB 430 Trillion (from estimates made by people inside China's property sector), which is about US$64 Trillion (this is *over 470% of China's 2018 GDP*). For obvious reasons, Tian as the chief to a state-owned bank wants to downplay the size of the problem.

China's *per capita* GDP is only about 16% to that of the US, and China's total output measured by the GDP account in 2018 was about 60% to that of the US, yet with the current abracadabra height of prices in China's property markets, total valuation for all the properties in just the four most expensive cities in China at Q2 2019 exceeds the total price of properties in the United States at its current valuation.

This illustrates how surreally distorted China's property valuations are, and how much an average consumer in China, by just having purchased the household's dwelling condo, is being sucked dry by such extreme prices in the country's urban property market. The figures disclosed above, for Shenzhen (the city right next to Hong Kong) the median price for an average-size condo is 57.34 times that of the median annual disposable income of the city's residents.

Further, with those who have incomes that are much below the median income and hence will probably never be approved by a bank for any mortgage, they are not doing any better than the mortgage-slave households. In mid-2017, the ratio of median rental costs to median dispensable income in the three most expensive cities aforementioned is Beijing: 58%, Shenzhen: 54%, and Shanghai: 48%. (these are the so-called first-tier cities) while in most second-tier cities this ratio is often near or above 35%. Hence, either owned or rented, housing costs eat away a huge chunk of ordinary households' disposable income.

All these figures portrait how disproportionately high China's property prices are, and how that eats into an average consumer's disposable income. The key macroeconomic issue here is, such abracadabra valuation negates the consumption component in our macroeconomics   GDP equation - the figures aforementioned necessitates the presence of severe short-changing in discretionary consumption with *middle class* household consumers and, crucially, *dragging down the all-important multiplier effect* - what's most fundamental to the economy's growth potential in China's current-stage macroeconomic configurations - where the investment-driven growth module has already created such a gargantuan pile of debts, amounting to a curse to the nation's growth potential. And, with the effectiveness of Beijing's monetary and physical stimulus policies proving fast diminishing.

Chapter 7

Not "Too Big to Fail", but "Too Big to Save"

What denouements are on the cards?

What was quoted earlier from the top-echelon insider in China's high finance sphere, Levin Y. Zhu, is key to our coming to grip with the underlying nature in China's development model. Zhu revealed in 2018 that *in the China model of development, with each one trillion GDP created, comes along a 6 trillion of incremental debt.*

Zhu, who obtained his Master's degree in accounting in 1995 from De Paul University of Chicago, with his having been inside the top echelon of Beijing's statecraft, is arguably one of the most qualified people in telling this truth - one that's unbeknownst to people the world over.

Noble Prize laureate economist Paul Krugman once commented that China is "not too big to fail, but too big to save". This author intends to help to substantiate such claim, with the following facts - to more usefully put things in perspective.

Here's what'll help you to dispel disinformation you've got from those China-Miracle Mongers on Wall Street.

- **There was nothing that's ever "miraculous"**

Those journalistic portraits depicting China's development in recent decades as an "economic miracle" are patently ignorant of (what's in more enlightened economic modeling, called) exogenous variable predicates in context, uniquely in the China case:

First, in how much of the growth was made possible by a thing that's institutionally unique of the country, the practice of State Landlordism - as to how lucrative it is to local government finances, for longer than the last 2 decades.

Secondly, in how the tremendous (what's called in development economics) Hirschman Linkage Effect in China's economy was brought in by the hundreds of thousands of manufacturing firms from Taiwan, having relocated their production base to China since the early 1990s, and what conglomerate bonus this has generated, entailing manufacturing firms all around the developed world to flock to China to set their manufacturing bases.

We will now deal with the first of the two factors above, as a first step to how such lucrative monetization of state lands is now coming to an end.

To start seeing how much has the monetization of state land helped to bring about China's past GDP figures, one is to know first, of the fact that (on average) circa 50% of the property price paid in any purchase goes to the governments' coffer, through the sale of (the right of use for 50 years) the state land, and the myriads of fees attached to property development on the land.

As it turns out, after being a mainstay GDP-booster for longer than two decades, China's state landlordism and its collusive modality in collaborating with property developers have already *crowded out* many options essential to the nation's more viable macroeconomic pathway. Local governments have collected about half of all the proceeds from the sales of property at the disproportionately high price and built all around the country gargantuan amounts of white-elephant public works - such that in the local-GDP-assessed bureaucratic system the local officials all got their promotions (or at least get to stay put, at their incumbent positions).

Such is a "growth by organized irresponsibility" model of China's, that have for the last 2 decades produced high GDP figures for show, to the world. And the underlying reality in all these: gargantuan amounts of grossly underutilized (some are outright utterly wasteful) public works and empty buildings and condos did create China's GDP figures we have seen in the past two decades. Then unpropitious macroeconomic consequences from these have in recent years started to reveal themselves.

Only after we have entered Round One of the US-China trade war, people have come to realize how China's technology industry could be not much more than paper-thin in many critical junctures: how easily the entire supposed-to-be hi-tech business viability of China's can vanish in the advent of American embargo - imposed on key components onto China's tech-sector corporations. If one keeps abreast of what's in China's industrial development, one sees how the prospect of China's employment situations have now quickly grown so much dimmer.

Then one starts to see what parallels there are, as exogenous variables (the jargon used in science and economic modeling, to mean variables whose values are determined outside of the system's determinations-within) that proved to have made the opportune moments for the economy to thrive in past decades now reversing their directionality.

- **The quantitative superiority in the debt-driven GDP - a Bolshevik mentality**

Let's reflect on what one of the most knowledgeable insiders of China's sphere of high finance, Levin Zhu, has revealed about the GDP-boosting modulation that's been at work for longer than the past two decades (mentioned in Chapter 1): *in the China model of development, with each one trillion GDP created, comes along a 6 trillion of incremental debt.*

The financing power attained through monetizing the state land has been one of the key exogenous variables that enabled China's dirigiste GDP-boosting feat we saw in past decades. Such power of financing is so uniquely endowed, as in China, the state owns *all* the lands of the nation - well, China's Constitution says all lands in the nation is owned by "the people", but that's nothing more than mere rhetoric (as you may know).

And, to people who don't know much of what the systems in CCP-ruled China's are about, it may be a big surprise when you hear that, such modality of the GDP-boosting contrivance has actually in it, the heritage of a Stalinist mindset - in how the Soviet fought the war against Nazi Germany. That is: how one of the most-brutal collectivist system triumph over the other most-brutal collectivist system, by the marshaling of sheer *quantitative superiority* - Stalin won the war by over 3 times the casualties in the Red Army (to that of the Nazi's in the eastern front), and having built the T-34 tanks numbered many times to that of all the German tanks in the eastern front.

In case you have not had a chance to become quite knowledgeable about this: the

Chinese Communist Party (CCP) is virtually running everything with a Stalinist mindset of war, including how they see the economy is to be operated. As this author has been involved in international business consulting relating to China for longer than the last two decades, he is qualified to inform you of such telltales.

To people who are not familiar with this piece of history: After Stalin's death in 1953, the Soviet leadership then denounced Stalin for his unsurpassed treacherous brutality. That caused Mao, the avowed Stalinist, to scorn the Soviet "Revisionism" - and hence the start of a most significant geopolitical shift in the world, wherein, from Nixon onward, lies the commencement of the (then) new era of White House's China policy - much to the benefit of Beijing's.

Now recall what this author had shown you earlier: for the last two decades, China's broadly defined money supply, M2, has been growing at an average rate of about 20% per annum, which is much more than twice that of the average annual GDP growth rate. Then relate this to what was said about the Stalinist strategy in WWII, of winning the war by sheer *quantitative superiority* - with a mindset of "couldn't care less about casualties". The 'casualties' (middle-class households that are now having to downgrade their consumption, and will be sunk into negative equity if the property market collapses) from China's hyperinflation in property prices are high, and (you know it) all consequences are to be borne by the common folks, surely by no means any of the CCP officials.

One phenomenon that helps you to visualize how the entire system of China's is the remotest one, from what can be called an equitable system. High-ranking officials in Beijing have all their food supplied by the "special provision farms": they never have to worry about the ubiquitous safety and health threats pervading food supplies in China (thanks to slack food-safety administration) - there are the pervasive overuse of pesticides for crop-growing and hormones in animal feeds that pose health threats the ordinary people face every day.

Arguably, the Soviet Union may not have won that war the way it has, without also the type of logistics and supply superiority predicated on the enormous supply of resources and trucks from the US at the time.

Ironically, we also have here a parallel between what the role the US played in early 1940s with the Soviet Union, and what that has been with China in the last two decades, in that the CCP's strategies in developing the economy would not have been what it is, without the tremendous help from all those self-serving investment bankers on Wall Street.

Remember what this author has shown to you earlier, of how in June 2017, Goldman Sachs' CEO posted on Goldman's own website a 3-minute video clip "China: Confidence on the Rise". One more instance for the fact that there is nothing (most of the) money managers on Wall Street wouldn't do, just to advance their personal gains.

- **A primacy macroeconomic parameter**

The unpropitious undercurrent in China's economy is visualized by seeing the cluster of Party-State economic entities, entitled to all sorts of prerogatives, making them *'not subject to the discipline of the market'*. Such is the institutional predisposition that helped to necessitate the macroeconomic 'curse' of a dwindling key parameter called the Marginal Propensity to Consume (MPC), and hence the shrinking of the multiplier effect.

For readers who have never studied the most basic course in economics, there is a brief introduction to this MPC and multiplier effect concept in the book's Appendix.

Unfortunately, this key issue of a weakening multiplier effect seems not having been identified by existing economic researches on China for its centrality. The likely reason for this is, as our mathematical model in macroeconomics was formulated *in ways that apply only to a genuine market economic system*. In such system, possible behavioral irrationality with economic agents' undertakings, in what the Austrian school of economics called *malinvestment,* is not given any parametric consideration, as they will be trivial in a genuine market economy - as, every business entity in a genuine market economy is subject to the discipline of the market. The big issue that most economic researches on China have not been given due consideration, is that such Austrian-School depiction of *malinvestment* is center, left, and right in China's Party-State economic system.

This is because, in a genuine market economy where the *discipline of the market* governs behaviors of all economic agents, such irrational behavior will never amount to an aggregate that's big enough, to substantially short-change the factors of injection in the macroeconomic circular flow. Demonstrably, a majority of economic researchers on China's economy have not been aware of the important fact of, how *institutional heterogeneity in the case of China may render our macroeconomic model an overly deficient representation* when said parametric consideration is not being visualized for its centrality.

That is, how the part of China's *not-subjected-to-market-discipline* setting could make our mathematical representation of the circular flow a grossly implausible one, when substantial deviation (owing to such institutional factor) with the *linchpin parameter of MPC* is not given its due calibration. That is, as China's economic system is far from a genuine market economy, in a Party-State system such *malinvestment* has been pervasive. And cumulatively, after decades, the denouement of outsized indebtedness has now presented itself as **growth-denying sinkholes.**

The case of China needs to be characterized by an exogenous, institutionally determined, *discounted parameter value* for its MPC. That is, *as the gargantuan aggregate malinvestment necessitated a short-changed factors of injection in the macroeconomic circular flow, the increase in aggregate demand by any GDP growth needs to be discounted by a percentage commensurate to the total interest expense incurred from existing debt repayments economy-wide.*

With the former Soviet Union, it runs a straight-forward non-market economic system, the gargantuan *malinvestment* was with the building of all the tanks and missiles. In the China case, it is with all the tens of millions empty condos, a plethora of ghost cities, ghost industrial parks, white elephant public works, and a high speed rail network now sitting on a debt pile of over three-quarter of a trillion US Dollar year after year, with a total revenue generated from its current operation that's far from sufficient in paying even the interest cost incurred from said debt liability.

One of the cornerstone legacies of Marshallian economic analysis is: among all possible market structures, monopoly creates the gravest deadweight loss to society. The Party-state system is an extreme type of monopoly, i.e., the Party is there to monopolize everything - hence it creates the extreme type of social deadweight loss. In the name of "reform", China has since 1979 evolved into what it is today, but for longer than the last two decades, what Beijing has practiced can only be realistically characterized as formulating the mainstay in the economy *a monopolistic economy that's of, by, and for the bureaucrats*. The macroeconomic consequence to this: a dwindling multiplier effect negating the economy's growth potential.

Independent observers like Capital Economics, a consulting firm in London, has earlier this year projected that going forward, China's annual economic growth may drop to 2% in future. This author points out, as a prevalent estimate with China's own economic research have had a consensus that, for every one point drop in the GDP growth rate there will be an increase of 8 millions in unemployment. Should such estimate being reasonably plausible, Beijing will not allow the GDP growth rate to drop below 4%. So you may never see China's GDP growth go down to 2%, what's a lot more probable is, to prevent such scenario from taking place, Beijing's measures will likely entail the coming of an era of stagflation.

- **The end of lucrative State Landlordism and the looming-large local government fiscal debacles**

In Q2 2019, all but one, among all the 22 provinces and 4 supra-municipalities are in very large budget deficits, relying on the central government to subsidize for their fiscal outlays. Even with the one and only local government that's not (yet) in red, the Shanghai municipal government has only very marginally a surplus, to less than 5% of the budget amount. A   local government fiscal debacle is in the making, with the officially disclosed US$ 6 trillion local government debt pile presenting itself.

What this local government finance Great Leap Backward signifies are:

1. The end of lucrative State Landlordism.

2. The day of reckoning has come, for Beijing's breach of good faith, with the promise made when joined the WTO in 2001 as a member, to transform the country's economy to a genuinely market-based one in a time span of 15 years. Consequential to this breach was the start of the trade war in Q2 2018.

3. The ultra-high prices in property markets have tremendously helped to lift all costs for the manufacturing firms, together with the prospect of China's experts being now subject to much higher tariffs, foreign firms have since 2017 started to exit China in droves, with the second cause further expedited the trend throughout 2018 and further accelerated into 2019.

For much of the past decade, state land sales (for the 70-year right to the use of land) plus taxes and fees charged to property developers (which in turn were transferred to the property prices, for all the mortgage-slave household to bear) have accounted for more than 60% of the local government revenues. Seen in 2018 was the start of a trend, of increasing number of failed state land auction, as a vast majority of property developers are now heavily in debt.

As was quoted in Chapter 1, the late-2018 S&P's assessment on China's local government debts: "The actual level of off-balance-sheet Chinese local government debt could be several times more than what is publicly disclosed,... (to be as high as) US$5.78 trillion". This figure is close to 50% of China's 2018 GDP.

Why is the system of state land monetization aforesaid having created a major price distortion economy-wide? For decades, all property developments in China starts with the collusive dealing between the local government and the property developer (whether state-owned or privately-owned firms). The local governments sell the right of use of land (don't forget that in the CCP-ruled China, all lands are owned by the state), unbeknownst to people who have no in-depth knowledge about how China's property markets operate, much of the obscenely high prices come from the part of China's property market that's *"not subject to the discipline of the market"*. It is a known fact, that some 70% of the cost in a typical property development goes to what's paid for (the right of use, of) the land, plus all the taxes in developing the property. And afterward, the system is also highly permissive of the developers' various ploys to jack up the price. In the end, typically in the eventual prices paid by home buyers, some 50% went to local governments' offers. This State Landlordism and its related institutional besetting - local government finances being highly reliant on land sales and a multitude of taxes related to property development - have contributed from the start, in making China number one in the world, in housing unaffordability indices.

China's is an amorphous system where undue influences come to negate the existence of accountability. Public resources are easily hijacked to serve the "gain privatized, and loss socialized "crony allotments in all shapes and forms. Economists in the west generally fail to understand how high property prices being an important means in China's local government finance through the commoditization of state lands. When you get to know enough about the system, you will be able to see that it is by and large no different from what's in a robber-baron type of a medieval system.

Superficially, rural lands are "collectively owned" by peasants. This doesn't mean very much when you understand that in a system where there is the total absence of anything that can be called the Rule of Law, and the administrative power of the Party-State is the only determination with everything. A commonality in the past two decades has been, the local government conscripted rural land bordering the urban area, from the peasants, at a price that's something like 1 to 5% of what the local authority will then sell (the right of use with) the land to property developers.

What is meant by "the discipline of the market"? It is, unsound investment decisions will incur the detriment of loss to those who made the investment decisions. In China's institutional milieu, collusive dealings between local governments and property developers are always immune to any such "discipline of the market". The now-pervasive 'mortgage slaves' phenomenon was necessitated by this kind of dyspraxia in China's semi-market economic system.

Failed urban land auctions are nowadays increasingly common. Local government indebtedness in some worst cases have been revealed by the news that some local authorities in medium and small city government have failed to come up with their employees' pay for months, every now and then.

- **What's formulaic of a debilitating mix**

Substantial proportions of China's past GDP figures were created by the herculean contrivances now prove to 'backfire', a cluster of things came consequential to Beijing's expediency-driven policies in the last two decades now come to fundamentally negate China's long-run macroeconomic outlook.

Reportedly, signs in the economy now evidence the diminishing return in the growth-stimulating effects from expansionary monetary and fiscal measures implemented in recent years, and for reasons that this book will demonstrate, that rate of diminishing will continue to keep apace. Some online forums in China dubbed this phenomenon as the economy's increasing "drug dosage resistance". While stimulation measures facing diminishing effectiveness, gigantic indebtedness incurred by a majority of corporate entities and local governments continues to pile up - for an absolute majority of these entities the only way for them to sustain is nothing other than rolling over - borrowing new debts to pay for the old ones when they fall due.

In 2018, the US GDP and money supply (in terms of M2) are (in Trillions of US Dollars) 20.2 and 14.42 respectively, while China's GDP and M2 are (circa): 13.8 and 27.99 (in Trillions of US Dollars). That is, China, with an economy that's about 65% in size to the US economy, had its central bank issued a money supply (broadly defined, as M2) that's more than 194% to the US counterpart. Much of these end up to infuse the enlarging China's gigantic property market glut and myriads of white-elephant public works.

The last five years have seen a trend of the rapid increase in China, of firms in the manufacturing industries, abandoned their core business (where profitability has been shriveling), cashed out and put the proceeds to join up in the titanic property market speculation of the nation. Such is one more aspect in the substantial furtherance of extreme financialization in the economy.

The prevalence of such modulating for ultra-valuation in the property market has given the effect of perpetuating a distortion in the matrix of macroeconomic parameters. In just the 3 years from 2014 to 2017, total household mortgage loans have doubled. The banking system's 2017 mortgage loans amount in the nation was already 300% to that of the total landing to all manufacturing industries.

The sum total value of China's property nationwide in the first quarter of 2019, of an estimated RMB 430 Trillion, amounts to nearly 500% of China's 2018 GDP. To see how outsized this mirage property valuation is, compare the followings: prior to the property and stock market collapse in 1990, Japan's nationwide property valuation was about 200% to its GDP. This figure, prior to the 2007 US subprime crisis, was about 170 %.

To reiterate the central theme of this book is: what caused such mirage valuation unprecedented in human history and how such extremity in price distortion necessarily entails debilitating macroeconomic consequences in terms of the economy's growth potentials. That is, even though China's Party-State economic system is, quite likely, capable of preventing a collapse of the property market, the serious deficiency in ordinary households' discretionary consumption entailed by such extremity of incommensurate housing burden is sufficient in bringing down GDP growth and increasing unemployment figures in fundamental ways.

Chapter 8

A Great Leap Forward of China's foreign debts

China's foreign exchange reserve crisis that you don't hear reported by mainstream media - China is now carrying a circa US$ 2 Trillion foreign debt

The apparent book value of China's foreign exchange reserve that Beijing wants to show you, of (circa) US$ 3 trillion, is deceptive - it is not the *balance sheet* value that you need to see.

For the first time in 15 years, the sufficiency of China's Foreign Exchange Reserves is now in serious doubt, the significance in this is in the foreign reserves' critical role in maintaining macroeconomic stability and the efficacy in implementing monetary policies. At the end of April 2019, for the first time in a decade, China's four major-league banks' net foreign assets in their books are negative.

The phenomenal shift (for the worse) in this bit of the financial health of China's economy is evidenced by the fact that China's foreign debts have from 2017 to the first quarter of 2019 increased by a whopping 35%. This sharp increase, a big chunk of it were incurred through the issuances of overseas corporate bonds by large firms in China. This was engineered by Beijing for the purpose of boosting the figures in China's dwindling foreign reserve account.

By the end of 2018, China's total foreign debts have reached the new height of US$ 1.965 Trillion, an amount that was unimaginable just a few years ago when Beijing was bragging about its foreign reserve being close to 30% of the national GDP (e.g., in 2016). In comparison, in Jan. 2019, China's foreign reserve amounts to only 22.7% of its 2018 GDP. While foreign debts now stand at close to two-thirds to the circa 3 Trillion foreign reserves.

- **The drying-up of foreign reserves and *a Great-Leap-Forward* of China's foreign debts**

Taking into consideration the portion in the foreign reserve that's subject to currency conversion by foreign firms that are entitled to the amount of their original amounts foreign direct investment when they first set up operations in China in earlier years, plus the nearly US$2 Trillion foreign debts now China is facing, the amount of foreign reserves that Beijing is able to mobilize is precariously limited - given the circa US$ 240 billion each year needed for the imports of oil, foods, and HI-tech components, these are indispensable imports.

People, in general, have only seen from the official statistics that China has at the end of April 2019 a foreign reserve of circa US$ 3.1 Trillion, what you don't see is that the part of China's foreign reserves that is actually at Beijing's disposal is only around US$ 400 billion. Taking the aforesaid US$ 240 billion requisite amount for the indispensable imports of energy and food, the foreign exchange reserve that Beijing could muster is to the tune of a sheer US$ 160 billion. For a nation of a population that's nearly 1.4 billion, this is a rather precarious thing.

To make sense of this, China needs to import each year about US$ 120 billion worth of Hi-tech components, foods, animal feeds and other commodities.

For the Hi-tech components part, there is no alternative sourcing other than from the US and Japan. The fact that more than half of the low-end manufacturing has already moved to South and South-east Asia, China's imports from US and Japan for hi-tech chips and other components for China-made cell phones and other electronics are indispensable. So is with energy, foods, and animal feeds - about 20% of food consumed in China are now imported. As China's energy productions are always far from self-sufficient, and today China can no longer produce enough food and animal feed. Efficiency in agricultural production has never had any meaningful lift in the past 3 decades.

Said fast increase in China's foreign debts were brought about by the prevalence of the untoward modulation of expansionism, depicted by Xiang and Zhu in earlier chapters, practiced in China's corporate realm, with the corporate issuance of overseas debt instruments.

Back in 2015, China's foreign reserves was at its height of nearing US$ 4 trillion, accelerated RMB depreciation in 2016 caused two things to make this figure to go down about an entire US$ 1 trillion: China's central bank intervention in propping up the RMB exchange rate, and the occurrences of capital flight through fake international trade transactions, which is the only way for people in China to move large amounts of money overseas.

From 2016 to 2018, there's been the continuation of China's trade surplus with the world for amounts that are larger than US$ 300 billion each year, but China's foreign reserve has not gone up at all. At the end of the first quarter of 2019, the figure stands at US$ 3.1, virtually no change from 2016. What this tells you is, for the 3 years to the end of 2018, Beijing has squandered huge amounts of foreign exchange on things like the One-Belt One-Road projects and other Great Leap Forward type of "Think-Big" things that turned into "Sink Big" things.

- **Mitigating a common illiteracy regarding how the financial markets work**

One needs to *dispel a common misconception propagated nowadays, regarding the US treasury bonds that China holds.*

In April 2018, an article published on CNBC titled "China's $1.2 trillion weapon that could be used in a trade war with the US", the arguments made in this article are fundamentally erroneous. It is based on a common misconception regarding how China may dispose of its holdings of the US treasury bonds.

The argument that China's US treasury bond holding is a "weapon" that Beijing can use in the trade war is, in reality, equivalent to a child's view of how the financial markets and asset valuation work. Anyone who knows financial trading well is able to tell you how laughable such an argument is.

First, if a large quantity of US treasury bond is being sold for non-price reasons at any day in the global bond market (traders of bonds are all professionals working for banks and other large financial institutions and they'll be able to tell this kind of sell is motivated not by where the price is at), it will cause the bond price to drop - what economics 101 tells you, when supplier curve shifts to the right (that is, quantity supplied increases for non-price reasons) and there is no significant change in demand, price will drop. So the seller next day will have to sell at a lower price for the same bond. And, it will take weeks for the $1.2 trillion bond getting sold, the seller who wants to sell a significant portion of the $1.2 trillion worth of the US treasury holding is simply acting out to *'shooting oneself in the foot'*.

Bonds are traded at a discount to its par value, reflecting the specific bond's set coupon rate and the supply-demand conditions at the time of trading. That dictates the inverse relationship between the price and the yield of the specific bond.

Secondly, as was articulated earlier, if you subtract the US$ 2 Trillion foreign debts that China now owes the world (a big chunk of these are from US lenders) and what is accrual, for Beijing to reimburse foreign exchanges to foreign firms that are exiting China (which is a significant amount each year these days) for their initial foreign exchange amount brought in to China years ago, from that superficial $3 trillion book value of China's foreign reserve that Beijing shows you, the amount of foreign reserves that Beijing is capable of mobilizing is less than $400 billion. And these are barely enough for China's must-have imports of energy, foodstuff, and other raw materials each year (China today needs to import 20% of its food, for everyone in the country to have enough to eat) - there is even no room here for the more than $100 billion imports of high-tech intermediary goods (such as IC chips and components that China cannot make) needed for the making of cell phones and other electronics goods.

● **Indebtedness, the institutionally-predisposed causation**

The institutional determinants that have helped to bring in all these predicaments need to be identified as, China's is a case of institutional dyspraxia, in this Party-State economy, things are being run by a fundamentally inequitable system of incentives. An institutional linchpin in this is a system of financial cronyism characterized by what we call the working of *adverse selection* in information economics.

Resulting from such institutional predisposition is an impaired market system where omnipotent vested-interest groups reap disproportionately titanic gains and *the talk of 'reform' has been, in effect, nothing much other than self-serving abracadabra* to further enrich the vested-interest groups in the Party-State.

The figure made known to the world, of China's corporate debts amounts to some 153% of the GDP is not likely anywhere close to reality. Some insiders in Beijing have in early 2019 revealed a much more startling figure: that China's total debts incurred by non-financial sectors have already in 2018 been nearing 300% to the nation's GDP.

This book points to how the multifaceted institutional factors are determinants that have shaped China's economic reality. Such institutional factors are what in our standard macroeconomic modeling categorized as *exogenous variables*, and they are largely left presumptuously unaccounted to, by the absolute majority of economists doing researches on China. Readers are to discover how a majority of economic research on China, with their ivory-tower type of methodology in economics, are blindsided by having gained no insight into how such *exogenous, institutional variables* are now at work, as the predispositions that shape the country's economic future.

China's heavy indebtedness is fairly well-reported nowadays, for instance, in "China's Debt Bomb" at Bloomberg, September 2018, author of the article quoted that some call China's debt problem "a treadmill to hell". This kind of journalistic hype just quoted do not get you to see much more than what's superficial. This book deals with what is underlying. It furbishes crucial insights gained from analyzing the intrinsic institutional causations. It demonstrates, as to what degree one could have been misled in picturing China's economy when relying on reports from a host of mainstream media. This book helps the readers to dispel all sorts of euphemistic paper-over when coming across a news reporting about China the next time.

What fosters the market-economy system in being the most efficient way for societies to organize economic activities is the working of the *discipline of the market*. With China's Party-State system, there are the colossal, forcefully self-serving Party-Cadre sectors entitled to undue prerogatives, *not subject to the discipline of the market*. This is the root cause for China's having accumulated in the last decade such gargantuan pile of debt, now rendered the nation's economy of the debilitating effect sketched in earlier chapters.

The types of indebtedness ailments are: the hundreds of millions middle-class household now having a monthly mortgage repayment that's much more than half of their disposable incomes. Property developer indebtedness - a plethora of 'ghost cities'. Local government indebtedness - a plethora of 'ghost industrial parks' (thousands of these across China) and white elephant public works. State-owned enterprise indebtedness - exemplified by a high-speed rail network now sitting on a debt pile of over three-quarter of a trillion US Dollars, with total revenue generated from its current operation that's far from sufficient in paying even the interest costs to service the debt.

● **An amorphous pseudo-market economy**

The Levin Y. Zhu quote mentioned numerous times earlier, that 6 trillion debts is required of one trillion GDP creation, is manifestation of what this author characterizes as China's institutional dyspraxia, and this is at the center in how China's amorphous pseudo-market economy of China's work.

Xiang Songzuo, an outspoken insider economist associated with one of China's top-three state-owned banks, in a January 2019 public speech quoted what Levin Zhu has depicted as the nature in how the gargantuan amount of debts were incurred, that they are inescapably consequential to *"The ubiquitous expansionism through undisciplined, sheer credit-creation means, permeated throughout local governments, corporations, and individuals. And this simply cannot be sustainable a thing."*

Levin Zhu studied accounting in 1994/95 at De Paul University of Chicago. He was named one of the Top 25 Most Powerful Business Leaders in Asia by Fortune Magazine (2004). He and his father were much responsible for the creation of the current Shanghai Stock Exchange in 1990.

Xiang Songzuo in that January 2019 public speech pointed to what's underlying (what he termed) *the pervasive, blind expansionism* in China's corporate undertakings. Xiang depicted for the *untoward modulation of expansionism* domineering in China's economy for longer than the past decade, elaborating on what he dubbed the *"malignant"* expansion:*"Corporations, in general, finance their expansions not predicated on their endogenous dynamism for growth, technological advancement, increase in profitability or retained earnings, but overwhelmingly relying solely on borrowings from the banking and shadow banking industries, as well as the issuance of corporate bonds that is now increasingly problematic"*. Xiang studied at Columbia University (N.Y.) in 1998-99, is one of the more knowledgeable academic figures in China.

The domineering of such untoward modulation for blind expansionism in the corporate and local government realms is the root-cause for China's current debilitating indebtedness. As such, how the debt piles were incurred also foreshadows how much all the overdrafts are intrinsically deleterious.

Two pivotal points worth highlighting here:

First, the fact that interest costs generated day by day, from China's existing debt piles has more than gobbled up the nation's incremental GDP of the entire year. And, the gap between the interest-cost-write-off to the year's GDP and the incremental GDP of the year, is enlarging. This has in it grave macroeconomic implications, as, the entire amount of the year's GDP increments were rendered the value of zero in the macroeconomic parameter of marginal propensity to consume (MPC) - as such incremental GDP amount was written off as the interest expense in debt repayments, it never gets to become anyone's income. Importantly, the in-depth connotation in our macroeconomic language from such occurrence is, this portion of the GDP that's to be assigned 0% MPC being larger than the year's GDP increment amount, and this drags down the economy's overall MPC, into one that's lower than the previous year's. This has been the case for 2018, then if said gap (where the year's total interest costs exceed incremental GDP) continues to enlarge, it translates to the diminishing of multiplier effect year over year. And, if a certain majority of the new loans are rollover loans, the pace of diminishing in the multiplier effect will continue to accelerate. This point will be further elaborated later.

Secondly, started from longer than a year ago, Beijing has secretively implemented measures such as having corporations to issue foreign debt instruments overseas, for the purpose of propping up China's foreign reserve figures.

- **Retrieving to the primacy macroeconomic parameter**

The undercurrent in China's economy is visualized by seeing the cluster of Party-State economic entities, entitled to all sorts of prerogatives, making them *'not subject to the discipline of the market'*. Such is the institutional predisposition that necessitated the macroeconomic 'curse' of a dwindling key parameter called the Marginal Propensity to Consume (MPC), and hence the shrinking of the multiplier effect.

For readers who have never studied the most basic course in economics, there is a brief introduction to this MPC and multiplier effect concept in the book's Appendix.

Unfortunately, this key issue of a weakening multiplier effect seems not having been identified by existing economic researches on China for its centrality. The likely reason for this is, as our mathematical model in macroeconomics was formulated *in ways that apply only to a genuine market economic system*. In such system, possible behavioral irrationality that economic agents may undertake, in what the Austrian school of economics called *malinvestment* is not given any parametric consideration, as they will be trivial in a genuine market economy. The big issue that most economic researches on China have not come to grip with, is that such Austrian-School depiction of *malinvestment* is center, left, and right in China's Party-State economic system.

This is because, in a genuine market economy where the *discipline of the market* governs behaviors of all economic agents, such irrational behavior will never amount to an aggregate that's big enough to substantially short-change the factors of injection in the macroeconomic circular flow. Demonstrably, a majority of economic researchers on China's economy have been aware of the important fact of, how institutional heterogeneity in the case of China may render our macroeconomic model an overly deficient representation when said parametric consideration is not being visualized for its centrality.

That is, how the part of China's *not-subjected-to-market-discipline* institutional setting could make our mathematical representation of the circular flow a grossly implausible one when substantial deviation (owing to such institutional factor) with the *linchpin parameter of MPC* is not given its due consideration. That is, as China's economic system is far from a genuine market economy, in a Party-State system such *malinvestment* has been pervasive. And cumulatively, after decades, the denouement of outsized bad loans have now presented themselves as growth-denying sinkholes.

The case of China needs to be characterized by an exogenous, institutionally determined, *discounted parameter value* for its MPC. That is, the gargantuan aggregate *malinvestment* necessitated a short-changed factor of injection in the macroeconomic circular flow, the increase in aggregate demand by any GDP growth needs to be discounted a percentage commensurate to the total interest expense incurred from existing debt repayments economy-wide. With the former Soviet Union, it runs a straight-forward non-market economic system, the gargantuan *malinvestment* was with the building of all the tanks and missiles. In the China case, it is with all the tens of millions empty condos, a plethora of ghost cities, ghost industrial parks, white elephant public works, and a high speed rail network now sitting on a debt pile of over three-quarter of a trillion US Dollar, with a total revenue generated from its current operation that's far from sufficient in paying even the interest cost incurred from said debt liability.

One of the cornerstone legacies of Marshallian economic analysis is: monopoly creates deadweight loss to society. The Party-state system is an extreme type of monopoly, i.e., the Party is there to monopolize everything - hence it creates the extreme type of social deadweight loss. In the name of "reform", China has since 1979 evolved into what it is today, but for longer than the last two decades, what Beijing has practiced can only be realistically characterized as formulating *an economy that's of, by, and for the bureaucrats*. The macroeconomic consequence to this: the dwindling multiplier effect that decimates the economy's growth potential.

Independent observers like Capital Economics, a consulting firm in London, has earlier this year projected that going forward, China's annual economic growth may drop to 2% in future.

As was articulated in Chapter 2, here the sum-up for how institutional peculiarity of China's will shrink the values of the macroeconomic multiplier, the key parameter as a major determinant in the economy's future growth potential, it is worth recalling here:

In our peculiar case of China, mainly 4 categories of institutionally-determined factors are bringing down the value of macroeconomic multiplier, and hence the economy's future growth potential:

(1). Hyperinflation in property prices lowers household *Marginal Propensity to Consume* (MPC) and hence short-change the household part of the *multiplier effect* economy-wide.

(2). The *financial caste system:* The SOEs get their loans from state-owned banks at the low-interest rates such as 5% - 6%, while privately-owned firms create more than 70% of all the urban jobs in China, the absolute majority of privately-owned firms generally don't get their loans from state-owned banks and need to pay very high rate of interest to borrow for their business undertakings, to the tune of 12% - 20%. This institutional factor brought in the macroeconomic consequence of as it causes a larger overall mark-up in price with goods and services and may also at the same time thinning profitability in the private sector, it shrinks the economy-wide macroeconomic multiplier effect.

(3) The *corporate caste system*: Low efficiency and arbitrary market power in pricing are characteristic of all SOEs and the communist-party-princeling-owned monopolistic business entities. The most egregious case in this being: logistics cost amounts to 18% of China's GDP, this figure is twice to that of the US. The main cause in this is the world's highest rates for superhighway tolls, in that all superhighways (being state-owned) are contracted to top communist party princeling cadres (sons of top communist party officials in Beijing), for them to set arbitrary toll booths on all routes across China.
Likewise, This institutional factor causes a larger overall mark-up in price with consumer goods and services in general, and may at the same time thinning profitability in the private sector. Thus it shrinks the economy-wide macroeconomic multiplier effect.

(4) Sales taxes and tariffs for imports are generally much higher in China than in any other major economies in the world, the extreme case in this is that if you buy a notebook (or laptop) computer in China, about half of the purchase price you paid goes to sale taxes.

- **The vaporized opportunity for the Lewis Turning Point**

Macroeconomic reality currently in China negates the occurrence of a crucial threshold in economic development called the Lewis Turning Point. Named after a key figure in the theory of economic development, Arthur Lewis.

Economic history illustrates the enormously important fact in the big picture: in the cases of Taiwan and South Korea, during the critical decades of the 1980s to mid-1990s, there have been sustained progression in both tremendous productivity gains and the narrowing of   gap between the growth rate in productivity and the growth rate in wages, resulting in continued commensurate enlarging of the middle class. What made the key difference in comparison, was that in the Taiwan-Korea case, for the relevant time period, urban property price hikes were never been to such egregious extent like what we have seen in China. The reason: as it is institutionally determined, there has never been comparable to so large a portion of the economy that is *"not subject to the discipline of the market"* like what's in the China case. The *amorphous pseudo-market system* of China's today is what makes all the difference.

Note: property prices have grown very high in Taipei and Seoul in more recent years, but they were not such disproportionately high relative to the average dispensable income at the time in the critical period of the 1980s - for there is to be a Lewis Turning Point to take place.

Conversely, in the China case, since 1983the gap between the actual productivity growth economy-wide, and the growth in wage rates has continued to widen (the growth in wage rates has continued lagging) for 25 years before 2014. Then, disproportionate high prices in housing mean that the increasing hefty burden in mortgage payment more than offset by far, any gain from the wage rate increases in China since the early 2010s. The claim of the alleged "Lewis Turning Point" has come to China some commentator made now prove emphatically false.

In the mid-1980s, urban populations in Taiwan and South Korea has already been more than 70%, while China today has an urban population that is only about 45%.

The extremity of high prices in urban property markets has rendered the needed urban-rural mobility a downright impossibility.

What Beijing has envisaged as, urbanization being China's next growth driver, now prove highly problematic, when even urban wage-earners are paying more than half of their income to just sustain a mortgage. The mortgage for an urban dwelling will be many times that of an ordinary income a peasant from rural areas can make, even working as a laborer in cities. Such proposition, that urbanization is to be the next driver for China's economy is fundamentally debunked by statistics revealed by one of China's 'indigenous' economists Zhou Tianyong, a professor in Beijing, who depicted that there will be *a 400 million rural population "sinkhole" in the consumption component of China's GDP*, for years to come.

This author concludes, side by side with Zhou's 400 million rural consumption sinkhole, there is *the more problematic 300-million urban "mortgage slave household" sinkhole* in the consumption component of China's GDP, for years to come.

Worse yet, when the tipping point comes, when such high price valuation can no longer be sustained, the plunging property market will amount to a perilous aggregation, where the hundreds-of-million-strong households who now self-perceived as the middle class will come to realized the fact that they are in actuality a member of the Negative-Equity Class.

This author points out, such macroeconomic predicament of China's today is destined in China's *institutional DNA*.

Appendix

For readers who have no knowledge in basic macroeconomics (or being 'rusty' in such knowledge).

This You Tube videos provides very good animated illustrations:
https://www.youtube.com/watch?v=lShcx6hLy24

For issues concerning MPC, this video gives a very intuitive visual presentation:
https://www.youtube.com/watch?v=RqWYmQQzXxs

For those who are more mathematically equipped, this video will be fun:
https://www.youtube.com/watch?v=czfJKPN-HEo

The multiplier Effect:
An initial increase in spending, cycles recursively (person A's spending is person B's income, with this income person B will spend a percentage (the MPC below) of it, and this spending becomes person C's income...) through the economy, resulting in incomes created that's multiple times larger than the initial dollar amount spent.

Marginal propensity to consume (MPC):
The proportion of disposable income (income after taxes) which individuals spend on consumption is termed the propensity to consume. MPC is the proportion of additional income that an individual consumes.

Factors that affect value of the macroeconomic multiplier:

The multiplier value will be higher if:
- Propensity to consume is higher
- Propensity to import is lower

- Taxes are lower
- The prevailing interest rate for business loans is lower

The multiplier value becomes lower if:
- Propensity to consume is lower
- Propensity to import is higher, one instance in this is when there are non-price causes for net exports to decrease, such as what are now in the US-China trade war
- Taxes are higher
- The prevailing interest rate for business loans is higher (higher interest cost eats into the firm's profitability)

As was summarized in Chapter 2, in our peculiar case of China, mainly 4 categories of institutionally-determined factors are bringing down the value of macroeconomic multiplier, and hence the economy's future growth potential:

(1). Hyperinflation in property prices lowers household *Marginal Propensity to Consume* (MPC) and hence short-change the household part of the *multiplier effect* economy-wide.

(2). The *financial caste system:* The SOEs get their loans from state-owned banks at the low-interest rates such as 5% - 6%, while privately-owned firms create more than 70% of all the urban jobs in China, the absolute majority of privately-owned firms generally don't get their loans from state-owned banks and need to pay very high rate of interest to borrow for their business undertakings, to the tune of 12% - 20%. This institutional factor brought in the macroeconomic consequence of as it causes a larger overall mark-up in price with goods and services and may also at the same time thinning profitability in the private sector, it shrinks the economy-wide macroeconomic multiplier effect.

(3) The *corporate caste system*: Low efficiency and arbitrary market power in pricing are characteristic of all SOEs and the communist-party-princeling-owned monopolistic business entities. The most egregious case in this being: logistics cost amounts to 18% of China's GDP, this figure is twice to that of the US. The main cause in this is the world's highest rates for superhighway tolls, in that all superhighways (being state-owned) are contracted to top communist party princeling cadres (sons of top communist party officials in Beijing), for them to set arbitrary toll booths on all routes across China.

Likewise, This institutional factor causes a larger overall mark-up in price with consumer goods and services in general, and may at the same time thinning profitability in the private sector. Thus it shrinks the economy-wide macroeconomic multiplier effect.

(4) Sales taxes and tariffs for imports are generally much higher in China than in any other major economies in the world, the extreme case in this is that if you buy a

notebook (or laptop) computer in China, about half of the purchase price you paid goes to sale taxes.

www.ingramcontent.com/pod-product-compliance
Lightning Source LLC
Chambersburg PA
CBHW020603220526
45463CB00006B/2425